D1554361

The Manipulation of Reality
in Works by Heinrich von Kleist

Cover vignette of Mohonk mountain silhouette
courtesy of the Publications Office, State
University College, New Paltz, New York.

Studies in Modern German Literature

Peter D. G. Brown
General Editor

Vol. 13

PETER LANG
New York · Bern · Frankfurt am Main · Paris

Robert E. Glenny

The Manipulation of Reality in Works by Heinrich von Kleist

PETER LANG
New York · Bern · Frankfurt am Main · Paris

Library of Congress Cataloging-in-Publication Data

Glenny, Robert E.
The manipulation of reality in works by Heinrich von Kleist.

(Studies in modern German literature ; vol. 13)
Bibliography: p.
Includes Index.
1. Kleist, Heinrich von, 1777-1811—Criticism
and interpretation.   2. Reality in literature.
3. Identity (Psychology) in literature.   4. Self
in literature.   I. Title.   II. Series.
PT2379.Z5G5   1987   838′.609   87-3055
ISBN 0-8204-0471-3
ISSN 0888-3904

CIP-Kurztitelaufnahme der Deutschen Bibliothek

Glenny, Robert E.:   .
The manipulation of reality in works by Heinrich
von Kleist / Robert E. Glenny. — New York;
Bern; Frankfurt am Main; Paris: Lang, 1987.
  (Studies in Modern German Literature; Vol. 13)
  ISBN 0-8204-0471-3

NE: GT

Printed by Weihert-Druck GmbH, Darmstadt, West Germany

for my parents

TABLE OF CONTENTS

PREFACE

This study is an examination of the private worlds and the public roles in which Kleist's characters exist. In choosing texts for this thematic study which explores the way in which Kleist's characters experience and relate to themselves, others, and the world, my selection was guided by several thoughts. First, in order to demonstrate that the subject of this study deals with a systematic pattern of Kleist's concerns, I wished to gain a reasonable cross section of Kleist's oeuvre, both from early to late works and also from the genres of both prose and drama. Further, I wished to take a more detailed look at works which by and large have not received their due in the critical literature on Kleist; these include Die Familie Schroffenstein, "Die Verlobung in St. Domingo," and to a lesser extent "Der Findling." Schroffenstein also has the virtue of being his first, even if not his best, work, and much of what appears in later works already occurs in well developed form in this play. The "Marquise von O...," on the other hand, receives substantial treatment not only because it is an excellent work which will always deserve new examination but also because it provides fruitful counterpoint to the discussion of the dynamics of other works.

With deep appreciation I thank Hugh Powell, Henry Remak, and Terence Thayer for their valuable suggestions on the content and argument of this work and for their critical insight into the problems presented by Kleist's texts. A special debt of gratitude is owed to Lawrence Frye for his generous giving of time and spirit to my work and for the care and depth of his thought. For their challenging thought in discussions about this study and about all my work, and for their invaluable assistance in preparing the manuscript for publication, I am grateful to John Kudlaty and Alice Reckley. I am also grateful to my students at Wabash College for their energetic willingness to run with and against my ideas, and to Jeff Qualkinbush, Stefan Kreischer, and Mark Schardine for their assistance in proofreading the manuscript. For financial support for the publication of this work I would like to express my gratitude to Wabash College and especially to William H. Sword for his interest in and support for faculty projects at Wabash College.

Crawfordsville   R. Glenny
February, 1987

Chapter 1

MIND AND REALITY

Critical thought on Kleist, as would be expected, has devoted a
great deal of time to the awesome task of describing, even ex-
plaining, the relationship of Kleist's individuals to their
worlds. While it has become the subject of considerable dispute
whether the individual should be viewed as a unified entity
absolute in its demands on existence, reality itself has been
routinely viewed as the implacable antagonist of the individual.
Regardless of how one defines the psychic structure of man in
Kleist's works, if one takes too facile a view of reality, one of
the essential problematic relationships in Kleist's works -- the
relationship between the minds of Kleist's characters and their
environments -- is bypassed. Those approaches which posit a
reality which foils man -- be it as inimicable fate, neutral
chance, intractable historical forces, or, as that convenient and
cryptic phrase would have it, "gebrechliche Welt" -- have already
restricted and directed the discussion of individual and reality
both in its content and its methodology, for man is then reduced
to volition and action, and the nature and validity of reality in
Kleist's worlds remains unquestioned.[1]

But before all human action -- and not only in Kleist's worlds -- comes the activity of consciousness, and many critics have wisely taken a step back and asked how Kleist's characters assess the reality in which they find themselves. This avenue of inquiry, however, has not been characterized by discussion of what knowledge means in Kleist's works but has primarily served to excite a debate, which continues yet today, on which organ of knowledge represents the proper means of attempting to know reality and the proper basis for action: feeling, reason, understanding, trust, dreaming, even autonomous self-consciousness, have variously been touted as the most accurate, the least accurate, or the only significant mode of psychic activity.[2] That these concepts have been hazily defined -- or not defined at all -- is only part of the problem encountered when trying to compare the arguments. But one might ask such questions as these: On what basis are these hierarchies of aspects of consciousness constructed? Just what is the difference, psychologically and practically, between trusting and feeling, or between feeling and reason, or between any two of these activities? Indeed, to what end do we make these distinctions central at all?

Ever since the critics have taken note of Kleist's Kant crisis -- or "cognitive crisis" if one prefers to avoid the controversy of whether Kleist misunderstood Kant or whether he misunderstood Fichte -- it has been recognized that there is a severe disruption in the ability of Kleist's characters to know reality as it truly is.[3] In the letter in question, to Wilhelmine in March, 1801, Kleist writes:

Wenn alle Menschen statt der Augen grüne Gläser hätten,
so würden sie urteilen müssen, die Gegenstände, welche
sie dadurch erblicken, sind grün -- und nie würden sie
entscheiden können, ob ihr Auge ihnen die Dinge zeigt,
wie sie sind, oder ob es nicht etwas zu ihnen hinzutut,
was nicht ihnen, sondern dem Auge gehört. (634, emphasis
Kleist's)[4]

Kleist's concern here is not with reality, but with pheno-

mena, the objects of experience: the crux of the problem, and

Kleist's interest, lie not in reality itself but rather in the

experiencing of reality. A second observation concerns that

relationship between phenomena and consciousness. Kleist com-

plicates the issue in a way by using more than one metaphor to

explain his concerns to Wilhelmine. The greenness supplied by the

lenses is used to illustrate the disruption in the correspondence

between object and object perceived.[5] But the operative metaphor

is really the eyes: the difficulty lies not in how things appear

to man but in what the eyes "do" to things. We must then above

all not begin by assuming that perception is a passive organ of

reception; the eyes are the metaphor for the mind going out to the

objects of its experience.[6] Kleist is using color as an easy

illustration, and the lack of correspondence between phenomena and

reality includes all phenomena, not just secondary qualities, such

as color, which are supplied by the mind.[7] Perception does not

function as a receptive organ, and this example illustrates the

problem of taking Kleist too literally. As the following

discussion will demonstrate, sight is only one way of experiencing

reality; there are others which are "faulty" as well. To

concentrate on sight or perception as the only cause for concern

here misses the point.[8]

Kleist places emphasis not on the objects but on experience. To derive the cognitive quandary of Kleist's characters from a tension between being and seeming, or between appearance and reality, is to set up a false dichotomy. That approach necessitates the position of an intact and unalterable reality which is encountered by a passive perceptual mechanism which by its flawed nature must fail. The concept of reality entertained by Kleist is not so simple, and in his worlds a far more subtle interdependence exists between reality and consciousness. Further, the notion that the perceptual mechanism fails leads to the suspect argument that a simple mistake, a <u>Versehen</u>, underlies the woes of the characters; and with that the search is on for a simple cognitive alternative to perception, the more basic activity of consciousness is bypassed, and the mind of the characters and their situation become obscured, even irrelevant.[9]

Instead, it is wise to ask the question that Kleist himself deals with in his many works, in his many worlds filled with very different characters with very different problems. How can man function in this crippling quandary? Indeed, how <u>does</u> man function in all these possible worlds into which Kleist casts his characters? Kleist may say in his letter to Wilhelmine that his highest goal is the search for timeless truth, but that by no means exhausts the problems of his characters who have more variegated, contingent, and immediate problems such as survival. As Karl Otto Conrady and others argue, Kleist's works have an experimental air about them in their delving into the question of how man can and should live in this world.[10] Our interest here is the mind of the characters in their attempt to exist, and indeed Kleist's writing serves to make the reader conscious of consciousness. For example, much attention has been drawn to the question of the reliability of the narrators in his novellas, and it becomes clear that we should not confuse the narration with the reality which is being narrated: the narrator is capable of shifting his vantage point from that of an external reporter to a locus in the interior of a character present at an event. Thus, in "Die Verlobung in St. Domingo," for example, Mariane is called "die treue Mariane"(175) because Gustav's thoughts are absorbed into the external narrative; Gustav's "teure Hand"(184) is so described not because it _is_ so, but because the narrator is eavesdropping on and fleetingly sharing Toni's feelings about Gustav, and there are other examples as well.[11] The narration in these moments occupies a place somewhere between objective narrative and interior monologue. The device, a rapid shift of perspective, does not present a reality but suggests, rather, an individual's way of ordering an environment. The narrative arrangement destabilizes and dis-integrates reality for us by creating a tension between events and the subjective inter-pretation of events, and this tension moves our attention to the minds of individuals who exist within an environment, and to their inner movements and ways of ordering reality.

Chapter 2

LANGUAGE AS ENVIRONMENT: THE BOUNDARIES OF CONSCIOUSNESS

It has become almost common wisdom that language fails Kleist's characters, by its very dynamic breaking down as a means of communication and expression. Hans Heinz Holz, who champions this view, finds the failure of the characters rooted in the failure of language itself. Seeing the novellas as being "bestimmt durch das Versagen der Sprache" and the dramas as demonstrating "wie Menschen an der Sprache scheitern," Holz argues that this failure of language is the central cause, not a symptom, of the fractured correspondence between truth on the one hand and representation and expression of reality on the other.[1] What underlies this position, with Holz and elsewhere, is the assignation of language to the world of appearances and to the denigrated faculties of reason or understanding.[2] But in approaching language in this fashion, language becomes oddly severed from the mind of the speakers; also, it is too simply assigned to a single mode of consciousness: reason. In Kleist's works, however, language is not so powerless as that nor does it bear such a simple antithetical relationship to truth. Both Holz and Müller-Seidel then see man as thrown back on ineffable feeling as the only way to know truth.[3]

It is obvious that Kleist's characters do not communicate well with one another, but the problem is not in language itself. The problem is in the closed and private nature of the personalities of the characters. They are seldom open to the world which surrounds them or to others. Kleist points out again and again that his individual characters exist in worlds that are different from the worlds of other characters -- different because the meanings of things and the relationships between things are different and private. Kleist also explores the relationship between the horizons of an individual's consciousness and the horizons of his or her language -- the linguistic space in which characters live.

Holz notes the restricted linguistic space in which some of the less complicated characters operate. In _Penthesilea_, for example, Odysseus and Antilochus quickly reveal that they have no words for the excessive, and undeniably irrational, behavior of Penthesilea. Their world is a simple world which falls more neatly into either-or possibilites of both actions and words. "So viel ich weiß," says Odysseus, "gibt es in der Natur Kraft bloß und ihren Widerstand, nichts Drittes"(125-6). And Antilochus certainly agrees with this assertion, both factually -- "Was sonst, beim Styx! Nichts anders gibts"(56) -- and linguistically -- "Ganz unerhört, ihr Danaer!"(122). Holz claims here -- since Penthesilea's behavior is irrational, both to us and to them -- that they must be viewed as the representatives of the faculty of reason and that the boundaries of their linguistic world are forced upon them by the boundaries of reason.[4] To make this type of systematic connection between reason and language, however, is unwise, for one ought not assume that Odysseus and Antilochus can be reduced to being merely representatives of the faculty of reason simply because they lack the emotional intemperance of Penthesilea. Likewise, it would be suspect to base a restricted linguistic world on the supposed limits of reason and come to the conclusion that language itself is woefully restricted. The limits of language lie rather in the limits of the mind itself and reflect the limits of the mind, for one cannot expect an individual's language to outstrip the mind which is content with the boundaries of its own ordering of the world; and Odysseus and Antilochus are certainly content with the bright world of war, as it is called in the play, which is simple by nature.

It is useful, then, to disabuse ourselves of the notion that language is defective in its very nature or is relegated to reason. Instead, it is more promising to look at the concrete functioning of language, at its power, at what language reveals about the characters' experience of themselves and of the world. In the "Marquise von O...," the first words of dialogue in the story come from the mouth of the Commandant, and already a great deal is suggested to us about the mental mechanics of the man. When the citadel at M... is being stormed by the Russians, we are told, "Der Obrist erklärte gegen seine Familie, daß er sich nunmehr verhalten würde, als ob sie nicht vorhanden wäre; und antwortete <den Russen> mit Kugeln und Granaten"(104-5). If one imagines the scene and statement, one is struck by its oddness, not so much as an opening line but as an unusual statement psychologically and situationally. That he fulfills his duty as an officer even though his family is present is not odd, but that he announces this, and in that way, seems so. It is neither a personal expression of a man to his own family, nor even, we note, a statement of duty, of what he must do, but rather something in between. The Commandant is suspended in that second -- as he is, indeed, in much of the story -- between his role as a family man and his role as an officer. His statement is, in fact, not a simple statement at all but rather a proclamation. He is not announcing how he will act even though his family is present but rather that he will act as though they were not present. It thus is somewhere between a negation and a statement of intent. The reason for this contradiction lies in the relationship between the Commandant and his utterance, in the relationship between his mind and his use of language.

Rather than going to his duty, the Commandant makes an almost ceremonial announcement which really represents a noisy shifting of mental gears, a mind in the moment of transition. The Commandant is speaking here primarily to and for himself, marking change to a different mode of behavior. The content of his mind is not clear to us, but we experience, through language, the status of his mind in the moment of transition. He separates, absolutely, his role as family man from his role as officer. He cannot be a family man and commandant, but only a family man or commandant. He does not, of course, destroy his family, but he linguistically negates them which clears the field for action. His words indicate that he is moving into a new mental environment, an environment which is quite real, which has different rules, and in which he has a different role. One senses in this brief description of him much that characterizes him throughout the novella -- his awkwardness in personal matters, the difficulty he has in expressing his feelings, the tension between social form and human feeling, and a rigidity of mind -- but behind all of these things, which one might call personality traits, lies a more basic power of consciousness that we shall see in many of Kleist's characters. The Commandant's mind alters his environment, blotting out his family linguistically -- as he will later blot out the existence of his daughter, and transporting him to a new role, which Kleist suggests thus: "und antwortete mit Kugeln und Granaten." As his speech is reduced, he shrinks as a person. While the military vocabulary incidentally serves to foreshadow succinctly what will become the dominant metaphorical system in the novella, its more important function is as a signal from Kleist about language and the mind, for it is not a military attitude, or "frame of mind" as one might call it colloquially, that is at issue here, but rather a framework of consciousness ready to supplant other frameworks of reality for the Commandant.

Linguistic worlds set aside whole areas whose existence is determined by language. This occurs again and again in Kleist's works, and not only with characters such as the Commandant who find themselves in complex emotional dilemmas. Even relatively simple characters such as Sosias in **Amphitryon** demonstrate this enormous capacity which language has. In the first scene of the play the "action" begins with Sosias creating an entire world through language, a world of heroic deeds in battle, a world into which he moves throughout the scene, a world created for the audience he will have with Alkmene, a world full of the minutest details based on no experience within reality. He becomes so involved in the spinning of the tale that imagination becomes confused with recall and he corrects his own "memory" of the details: "--halt! Mit dem Hauptkorps ists nicht richtig"(97).[5]

What Sosias speaks is not the truth, of course, which is made amply clear by juxtaposing his recounting of the events with his own characterization of the real author of the events, Amphitryon, who was not using language: "Er sagt wenig, tut viel, und es erbebt die Welt vor seinem Namen"(66-7). But the truth of reality need not correspond to and can have less importance than the experience of reality as it is posited through language. It may be a counterfeit world Sosias creates, but briefly it was truth for him and would have been truth for Alkmene who would have believed the illusion he creates. And the question arises in the play as to whether language ought to represent the truth in communication at all, for even the simplest of social "rules" may prohibit the expression of a particular reality, as Sosias, with the fool's naive wisdom, makes clear when he must report to Amphitryon later and, before he begins, wants to know whether he should speak truthfully or whether he should speak "wie es bei Hofe üblich"(625):

Sag ich Euch dreist die Wahrheit, oder soll ich
Mich wie ein wohlgezogener Mensch betragen? (626-7)

It is episodes such as these, and others -- not so comic -- which we shall consider shortly, which will make us reconsider just how important objective truth really is for Kleist's characters and how much they really desire it. For reasons which vary from situation to situation, words frequently seem totally independent of the things they pretend to describe.

Whole systems of order in reality -- affecting where, what, and how one is -- hinge on the word. Gustav, in the "Verlobung in St. Domingo," asks a Kleistian question, indeed, after Strömli tells him of the horrible blunder Gustav has made. "Oh ... ist das, was ihr mir sagt, wahr?"(193) This question is peculiar because of the notion that the truth of the words can actually be validated by the very speaker of the words -- especially peculiar in a story which has deceit and lies as the primary dynamic. Words are debased coinage in this story in which everyone, except Strömli, has lied. Gustav's question is not merely a cliche but a wish that there is a mistake here. He somehow hopes that Strömli has fabricated his accusation.

Words attempt to become their own guarantor, corresponding to themselves rather than to the stuff of reality they purport to represent. As another example of this, the Graf in the "Marquise" tries to create his own moral character as he neatly assures the family, "daß er, mit einem Wort, ein ehrlicher Mann sei," -- and he adds that same almost laughable closure of the statement upon itself, making the request -- "und die Versicherung anzunehmen..., daß diese Versicherung wahrhaftig sei"(112), as if a verbal re-

assurance of the truth of the statement somehow augmented its
veracity.

But in these examples -- the first, where Sosias' verbal
creation replaces experienced reality, and the second two, where a
self-supporting verbal system, "mit einem Wort," gains independence and tries to be a substitute for character -- language is
no laughing matter for the characters involved. The linguistic
worlds they inhabit and create are, literally, where they are at.
It is this that lends such importance to these linguistic worlds
in Kleist's works. They can overwhelm and supplant reality and
characters rather than remaining extensions of reality or character. Words cease to be signals and become essence and reality.[6]

It is striking in Kleist's works how intensely aware
characters are of their own and others' language, vocabulary, and
usage.[7] It is obvious that the language a person uses can reveal
who one is and what one thinks. Kleist, however, draws attention
to the way in which people's language can brutally be taken for
their essence. People in the works can become categorized by the
word, fixed instantly by the language they use, whether or not it
is appropriate or truly reflective of the mind of the speaker.
Gustav's problems begin with his words, words which are heard by
others, which run counter to the tide of revolutionary thought in
the Reign of Terror. In very practical terms, the possible
linguistic space in France becomes leveled and reduced as the
Revolution sweeps away and destroys all individual assertion or
expression not consonant with its own ethic. People there learn
to speak a language that contains only certain thoughts and

values. The rules have changed and he ignores them: "Gott weiß,
wie ich die Unbesonnenheit so weit treiben konnte, mir ... an
einem öffentlichen Ort Äußerungen ... zu erlauben"(174), he
laments much later as he sits in the middle of another revolution.
When he violated the political "rules" in France by blurting out
counter-revolutionary statements, he was forced to flee the
country; Marianne, of course -- by association with him -- is
removed much more thoroughly by the guillotine.[8] A similar
becoming-known through the word is obvious in that other work
where locating the enemy is of such crucial importance, Die
Familie Schroffenstein. The unfortunate minions of Warwand who
were found by young Peter's body seal their own wretched fate by
uttering the one word, "Sylvester," under torture. The one word
is the key which unlocks -- so the receiver believes -- the entire
world the individual inhabits, even though what the person is may
not correspond to the assumptions of the listener.

Language does not only reveal the content of a person's mind,
in any case. It is also a creative and active means through which
characters may demonstrate their own self-definition and world.
To return to Santo Domingo for a moment, near the end of the story
Babekan and Congo Hoango scorn Toni as a traitor. But Toni will
have none of that, for she thinks of the world and herself in an
entirely different way; she has started to re-name things: "Ich
habe euch nicht verraten; ich bin eine Weiße ..." (191). The word
"treason," by virtue of her new self-definition and viewpoint, can
no longer apply to her, she is saying, because she has moved to a
new category, that of enemy. Our attention is drawn to the

problem of perspective here, for no one would be likely to call himself a traitor. The label depends on where one is standing; for Babekan and Hoango it is a political problem, for Toni it is an existential concern. This is a subtlety which, under the circumstances, undoubtedly escapes Babekan and Hoango.

A person's language obviously can be indicative of his or her understanding of how the world itself functions, of what a character's world is. Kleist frequently juxtaposes personal worlds which are structured in radically different ways. It becomes apparent that for Kleist reality is not composed of things but is, rather -- in experiential and psychological terms -- a system of rules. In the opening scenes of <u>Schroffenstein</u>, two radically different systems of rules are presented. At Rossitz, in the impersonal choruses of boys and girls, an entire cosmos is described. God, nature, and man's relationship to man are included and related in somewhat less than twenty-five lines of text. One could write at considerable length on the images and their relationship in the choruses, but for this argument it is sufficient to note the representation -- on a hyperbolic, mythical level of innocence in harmony with God and nature, an innocence which has been betrayed and destroyed by a murderous enemy, a world which has been warped by the foe and is treacherous. Harmonious, neutral nature has been perverted by others, the environment literally poisoned. As Gertrude says to Agnes:

Du sollst mit deinen Händen nichts ergreifen,
Nichts fassen, nichts berühren, das ich nicht
Mit eignen Händen selbst vorher geprüft. (1238-40)

In the sketches for the <u>Familie Ghonorez</u>, this warning is made even more ominous in its sweeping exaggeration. Rodrigo pleads with Antonio to guard Ignez carefully:

> Die Blume, die sie pflückt, kann man vergiften,
> Drum koste, prüfe, untersuche alles,
> Was sie genießen mag, bis auf die Luft. (829)

Though it is the concrete incident of young Peter's death which occasions the spectacle at the beginning of the play and which, as the most recent escalation in the violent feud, hangs over the entire play, it is not actually an event. The alleged murder of Peter, which sets the play in motion and which provides the exposition at the outset is rather a linguistic paradigm for how the environment of the houses of Schroffenstein functions. It is not only a verbal model of how the world works but also a model for how the characters do or should behave, and it is this model which, as we shall see, really hangs over the entire play.[9] It is a model which is fixed, appropriately enough, by the word: a solemn oath is sworn and the hateful world portrayed in the opening lines becomes a binding plan for vengeance. Rupert exhorts all Rossitz to swear solemnly and individually to a single plan of action and to recognize a single enemy:

> Ein Fluch, wie unsrer, kömmt vor Gottes Ohr
> Und jedes Wort bewaffnet er mit Blitzen.
> Drum wäge sie gewissenhaft. (30-2)

More than Peter, this static model of language, of reality, of behavior and thought, is the setting and the motor for what ensues.

In fact, <u>Schroffenstein</u> is in many ways a tragedy whose course can be observed through the growing encroachment of this

model on the character of Sylvester. When he first appears, he
lives in a world in flux, a world growing, changing according to
human design, perfectible; he speaks of the ordering of the
garden, his domain, according to man's will(490-1). It is a world
in peace, in harmony, within control, where man is in nature and
nature in man. As he says to the gardener:

> Denk dir das junge Volk von Bäumen, die
> Wenn wir vorbeigehen, wie die Kinder tanzen,
> Und uns mit ihren Blütenaugen ansehen. (492-4)

But what happens with this garden which is, metaphorically and
really, his world, and what happens to this flowing system of
language where natural phenomena explain man and man is used to
explain nature in metaphorical terms? These things become lost,
overwhelmed by the march of the internally static world of fear
and vengeance which was established in the first scene of the
play.

We can follow Sylvester's "conversion" through the change in
his language. After he fails to defend the integrity of this
peaceful world, his view of his situation and of the rules of the
environment begin to merge with the position of Rupert of Rossitz.
The first sure indication is when Sylvester retrenches and issues
an exhortation to his people to defend themselves against the
enemy. He says, "Es geht für alles, ja, was heilig ist und hehr,
für Tugend, Ehre, Weib und Kind und Leben"(940). The content of
language has become frozen in defensive posture; the progressive
flux of the environment has become replaced, and Sylvester is
trapped within his own slogans. Further, one cannot fail to note
that his call is an echo of Rupert's call to Rossitz in the first

scene: "Ich biete euch, meine Lehensmänner, auf, mir schnell von Mann und Weib und Kind, und was nur irgend sein Leben lieb hat, eine Schar zu bilden"(63-6). The postures of their separate attitudes have begun to merge. Sylvester's order of the world becomes progressively supplanted; he adapts himself to the rules he sees before him. This is his tragedy -- capitulation and adaptation.[10]

Sylvester exchanges one role and world for another and vastly different world. It seems impossible for him to do otherwise. In one of the better scenes of the play, he stands quietly at the window, surveying the world:

> Es ist ein trüber Tag
> Mit Wind und Regen, viel Bewegung draußen. --
> Es zieht ein unsichtbarer Geist, gewaltig,
> Nach _einer_ Richtung alles fort, den Staub,
> Die Wolken, und die Wellen. (2019-23, emphasis Kleist's)

Compared to his earlier description of man's control over nature, this description, as a metaphor, shows him to have completely changed the way in which he thinks of reality itself: the rules of the environment -- of reality itself -- have changed, for the elements -- earth, air, and water -- are pulled in one direction. And Sylvester follows this pull. He adopts the attitudes he sees before him, those of Rupert. Rupert's first utterance in the play, "Ich schwöre Rache! Rache!"(23), is now echoed in Sylvester's self- and world-defining statement of reduced stasis, "--fortan kein anderes Gefühl als nur der Rache will ich kennen" (2055-6). From that point on, Rupert and Sylvester are virtually indistinguishable in their thought and actions. With the talk of vengeance and enemy, the content of Sylvester's consciousness is limited by the boundaries of this new arrangement of the world, and linguistic possibilities are leveled.

The system of language in which the characters operate is a clue to what a character is -- not only to the reader but also to other characters. Kleist's apparent attraction to trials, to interrogations, to inquisitions, to probing questioning, reveals not only an agonized searching for the nature of the others or for truth. The inquisitions themselves are often at the center of the matter and problem. It is the very testimony of characters which is sought; it is not so much a desire to hear information -- what is or what has happened -- but to discover and reveal the person by how he or she represents reality. It is the attempt to ascertain the order of the world in the person's mind through the verbal system, the world which his or her language circum-scribes.[11] We have already noted the supposed revelatory nature of Gustav's indiscretion and the unfortunate gaffe of Warwand's minions, but more systematic attempts are made to locate and define individuals.

The structure of inquiry and testimony underlies the beginning of Käthchen von Heilbronn. In the first scene, the purpose of Theobald's and Strahl's testimony before the vehmic court is not merely exposition, the revelation of what has occurred before the play begins. Like the death of Peter in Schroffenstein, the event under discussion -- Strahl's alleged "seduction" of Käthchen -- is entirely eclipsed by the testimony. Neither previous history nor action, it is, rather, the attempt by the judges to unlock the inner world of the speakers. It is a digging into the "Höhle der Brust"(4) more than a seeking of facts.

Theobald is the accuser, and he sets out to convince the judges of Strahl's guilt. But when the judges ask him to relate the reason for his charges, he begins neither with evidence nor with a relation of events, but rather he creates a hyperbolic vision of the cosmos -- angels, apparitions, God, the order of nature overthrown by devils, demonic forces and magic. He associates Käthchen with God's order and Strahl with the devil in a weaving of images and observations that do not begin to touch on the events that brought forth the charge. It is some 130 lines into the play before Graf Otto, after several attempts to direct the testimony to the facts, finally brings Theobald away from lengthy circumlocution and hyperbolic interpretation back to a narration of the events. In the meantime, however, Theobald's rhetorical strategy has also revealed the content and workings of his mind through the language he uses. He does not report but posits. Of Käthchen he says, in part:

> ... gesund an Leib und Seele, wie die ersten Menschen,
> die geboren worden sein mögen; ein Kind recht nach der
> Lust Gottes, das heraufging aus der Wüsten ... wie ein
> gerader Rauch von Myrrhen und Wachholdern! Ein Wesen
> von zarterer, frommerer und lieberer Art müßt ihr euch
> nicht denken, und kämt ihr, auf Flügeln der Einbildung,
> zu den lieben, kleinen Engeln, die mit hellen Augen, aus
> den Wolken, unter Gottes Händen und Füßen hervorgucken
> .... (65-73)
> ... das Käthchen von Heilbronn, ihr Herren, als ob der
> Himmel von Schwaben sie erzeugt .... (78-9)

Theobald's references to her, and there are others like these, come almost exclusively from the religious realm. References to

Strahl, on the other hand, too numerous to cite, are explicitly from the satanic and demonic. What is intriguing is that Theobald bypasses evidence in his charges. In Ciceronian manipulative twists of statements he makes accusations based on the content of his own statements, not on reality. Perhaps the best example of this:

> Ich sah den Satan und die Scharen, deren Verbrüderten
> ich ihn nannte, mit Hörnern, Schwanzen und Klauen, wie
> sie zu Heilbronn, über dem Altar abgebildet sind, an
> seiner Seite nicht. (52-5)

What strikes us is not so much his flight of imagination but rather the use to which he puts it: his ploy during this "testimony" is based on the creation of a reality through words, even though he must admit -- but not until the very last syllable -- that the statement is not fact. At the last he negates the statement, but the statement has been made; that reality is there. But his strategy fails, in part because he believes what he is saying about demonic forces and magic.[12]

The cosmos he posits -- nature being assaulted by demonic forces and its order being overthrown by black magic -- is rejected by the judges. However, it is the rules of Theobald's cosmos they reject more than his accusation. The judges operate on a different level of significance of words and events: they simply live in a different world than he does. Graf Otto sums up the judges' position at the end of the testimony: "Der aber-witzige Träumer, unbekannt mit dem gemeinen Zauber der Natur!" (613-4) Magic, as a word, functions in two spheres which do not coincide; in effect, it is not so much his charges which are rejected as his entire system of organizing the accusation.

In the opening trial scenes, Strahl goes about his defense in a related way. In interrogating Käthchen, he, too, posits realities that exist only insofar as they are expressed verbally. But Strahl's rhetorical strategy is different. Bypassing Theobald's initial accusation -- that Strahl exerts a supernatural and demonic control over Käthchen -- and restricting his statements to the plane of physical evidence, Strahl creates through irony fictional events which, if they were true, would indeed place some guilt on himself. Rather than directly establishing the innocence of his own actions, he repeatedly describes himself as having performed various and sundry nefarious acts and sequences of acts in space and time: he says that he drugged her, visited her in the stall and sent Gottschalk away in order to be alone with her, made suggestive remarks to her, attempted to embrace her, kissed her, beat her, set the hounds on her, and more. The tactic works, because even as each incident is created, Käthchen negates it: "Nein, mein hoher Herr," she says repeatedly(491, 496, 515, 575, 590, 597, 601). The end result is that, as the entire catalog of evil and culpable acts is posited and destroyed, a total vacuum of involvement in the events remains. Strahl establishes his innocence by removing himself -- or rather, by allowing Käthchen to remove him -- from the causal chain of past events.

In the court scene, two sets of representation are rejected -- Theobald's hyperbolic arrangement of reality because it does not at all coincide with the world the judges inhabit, and

Strahl's because it is negated as its facets are expressed. The truth -- what actually occurred -- lies somewhere in between but remains undiscovered. But as we have seen, reality may take second place to its verbal expression. There is, in fact, truth in Theobald's claim: natural order was overthrown; Strahl does exert a sort of magical control over Käthchen. But the truth remains to be seen later, by the characters and by the readers. The issue in the opening of the play, however, is, oddly, not reality. The search by characters is, just as in Schroffenstein, not for the prehistory of the play; a shift in focus occurs, from actual events leading up to the play's action to the realm of the word. It is not action which sets these plays in motion but rather the linguistic movement of the characters as they create order and define reality and character for themselves and for others. Space and time are shifted, altered, tampered with -- intentionally in Strahl's case, perhaps unintentionally in Theobald's -- and lose their importance as the ostensible center of our attention. Reality is not the issue, but rather the representation of it and the question of whether it will be accepted by others or not.

This is made clear in that other drama of testimony, Der Zerbrochene Krug. All the characters report on the events of the night in question, yet we learn that nearly all the events reported are alleged to have occurred at the stroke of eleven o'clock. The contradictory reports dealing with events that could not possibly have occurred simultaneously create a unique problem.[13] In effect, space and time become frozen, and we are left with only testimony to consider, i.e. the events as expressed by the characters in court. Testimony is in fact not only at the core of the form and structure of the play but at the core of the very problem of the play. Our attention is focused precisely on what people say, not on the events of that night, for Adam's guilt is apparent, to the reader at least, from the first scene, and Kleist does not allow the tension of the reader's not knowing who the culprit is to be an issue. The play is a war of perspectivistic representations of reality fighting each other for credence and acceptance through the word. In such situations as these it becomes highly problematic to speak of language as a tool of communication at all, much less to speak of a simple failure of language.

Chapter 3

THE CONTROL OF REALITY

More than one dynamic aspect of language in Kleist's works gains progammatic significance. Language can serve not only to show what one is and reflect what a person's world is. It is not only a tool of assessment; it can also serve as an instrument of control by means of which characters can attempt to posit who they are and what reality is. In many situations in Kleist's works, language is not autonomous, determining the individual by its rules. Rather, characters themselves can attempt to define themselves and create their environment. Clearly, language is closely linked with consciousness here, but it proves insufficient to think of language only in terms of what it can reveal about the identity of self. Rather, the practical workings of language demonstrate that it is itself a mode of consciousness, a way to go out to the world, to know the world through the word and thus fix one's relationship to it through the word.

This active aspect of language, a fearsome power, pervades Kleist's works. Language fails only in certain ways. It functions for individuals on different planes as it creates its own space, defines the essence of others, imposes order, and posits reality. The remainder of our discussion of language will focus on what use the control of the word is to the characters. As we have repeatedly hinted, through the discussion we shall see that a definition of truth as the correspondence between reality and its expression is of limited use when thinking about Kleist. The search for noumena, in the works and in Kleist criticism, may thus reveal itself to be a misplaced attack when approaching Kleist's characters.

The verbal confrontation between characters in Kleist's works frequently represents a transaction that has little to do with the normal functions of conversation. One is hard pressed to describe individuals' verbal expression in normal terms of discourse such as communication, compromise, discussion, or dialectic completion of perspective. The process of expression occurs on a very different level, a level as basic as the individual's experiencing of reality and the individual's necessity to have his or her ordering of reality confirmed in some way by the receiver of the words. There is frequently a feeling that if one controls the words, one controls the reality that the words purport to represent, and this feeling -- one can hardly call it awareness, because so much of this activity lies well below conscious thought -- forms the basic dynamic of many verbal "exchanges," forcing us to reconsider the very notion of words as representation.

On the level of subject matter of conversation and on the level of the manner of the presentation as an element of content, the attempt is made to control the flow of reality. One so often cannot escape the impression that characters are performing verbally -- for themselves and for others -- and that much hinges on the acceptance or rejection of the words themselves. Before the content is even formed into words, the form of the presentation may make a significant statement that determines the nature and importance of the conversation which ensues.

Representative of the first of a series of linguistic models which we will discuss is the attempt to manipulate the presentation and direction of discourse. When Graf F., for example, bursts into the Commandant's home, the shocking impact he has on the family is due less to his remarkable resurrection than to the bizarre, virtually complete lack of sense for proper social behavior which his entrance and opening words display. The speech of the family, indeed of the entire novella, proceeds on a highly stylized plane -- formal, elegant, subtle -- which emphasizes both the formalistic nature of discourse in the interactions of characters in the novella and the premium which characters in this novella -- a novella in large part about the breakdown of order -- place on the maintenance of form and order in their environment. That the maintenance of order is also of existential significance for the characters is a necessary corollary of this, of course, and will be discussed in later chapters.

The Graf's position in this scene is, for the moment, of less importance to us than the manner in which the Commandant and his family react to the unwonted intrusion and to the disruptive stress which the Graf's behavior causes. He enters, inquires after the Marquise's health -- and promptly appends the question whether she wants to marry him. The unheard of penetration through social form to the intimate sphere of Julietta's own world causes a stir, indeed. The Marquise blushes; the mother says nothing and is, we are told, embarrassed. Julietta looks at her mother who in turn looks at her son and the Commandant, in a silent search for a confirmation that the Graf's behavior is indeed improper. The norm of the community is tacitly reestablished through the glances, and the Commandant, with recovered grace, "obligingly" sets a chair before the Graf and asks whether he would not like to sit down. The mother changes the subject matter of "conversation" to an inquiry, in an equally elevated style, into the Graf's seemingly miraculous survival, whereupon the Graf sits down.

Within eleven lines a brief but fascinating encounter has occurred, circumscribing the temporary collapse and restoration of the order of things in the family's shared world. Obviously, greater shocks await them, and this scene, which represents the last effort taken in concert by the family until the end of the story, is merely a brief victory for their common grasp on reality before the near total disintegration of family and order. The exchange of glances among them is the silent defensive reassurance that their own expectations are indeed sound. After the Graf departs, the family, like a committee, unifies its impressions of the Graf and his attitude. They judge him "rasend"(117), the alternative being to release hold on their own world.

The Commandant's invitation to the Graf to sit down is a gesture which in context gains in importance, going beyond a mere gesture of hospitality. The assault on order by the Graf is countered initially not on the verbal level on which the Graf himself had begun. Rather, the Commandant declines to engage the Graf through the use of words at all. He in effect ignores the Graf's outburst, denying its validity as the stuff of conversation, and moves to a non-verbal, though hardly sub-communicative, level by offering the chair in an attempt to stop the scene from continuing in the same uncontrolled vein, to return to the forms of social courtesy, to start the conversation over again with different content, as the mother then attempts to do. An interesting aspect of the Commandant's gesture is that it is a wordless "amenity" that, if accepted, puts him again in control of the situation. Had the Graf not acknowledged or accepted the "simple" gesture, the stress on the Commandant might have been considerably greater.

Just such a refusal occurs both on the level of gesture and on the level of language in <u>Schroffenstein</u>, and it provokes a devastating reaction. In the second scene of the play, the herald, Aldöbern, comes to Warwand to accuse Sylvester of the murder of Peter and to declare a war of total destruction. But even before Aldöbern speaks, Sylvester is attempting to control the progress of events. One can perhaps detect an underlying nervousness in the forced jocularity of tone in Sylvester's long speech of welcome, as if he guiltily fears the words just passed between himself and Gertrude on the evil intentions of Rossitz somehow are still hanging in the air when Aldöbern enters the room. A confrontation between Rossitz and Warwand is something Sylvester desperately wishes to avoid.

In content, Sylvester's speech is an amazing verbal creation.
On the surface he may seem to be asking Aldöbern for his message,
but the whole presentation reveals itself to be an elaborate
suggestion for the content of Aldöbern's coming speech:

> ... setz dich zu mir, und
> Erzähle mir alles, was du weißt, von Rossitz. (561-2)

However, Sylvester has more specific ideas of what "everything"
means:

> Denn wie, wenn an zwei Seegestaden zwei
> Verbrüderte Familien wohnen, selten,
> Bei Hochzeit nur, bei Taufe, Trauer, oder
> Wenns sonst was Wichtiges gibt, der Kahn
> Herüberschlüpft,... (563-7)

Sylvester creates a simile that is a vision of a harmonious
relationship between two families, and he suggests the harmless
and positive nature of any possible message between the families.
All the images he uses posit and suggest a tone of common bonds,
communication, contact, and community, indeed, a common world. He
continues:

> ... und dann der Bote vielfach,
> Noch eh er reden kann, befragt wird, was
> Geschehen, wies zuging, und warum nicht anders,
> Ja selbst an Dingen, als, wie groß der Ältste,
> Wie viele Zähn der Jüngste, ob die Kuh
> Gekalbet, und dergleichen, das zur Sache
> Doch nicht gehöret, sich erschöpfen muß --
> Sieh, Freund, so bin ich fast gesonnen, es
> Mit dir zu machen. -- Nun, beliebts, so setz dich. (567-75)

This is an attempt to guide and supply the actual content and
form of Aldöbern's imminent message by suggestion. But, of course,
it fails completely. His insistent and repeated offer to Aldöbern
to sit down is ignored. Here the minimal request to establish a
common agreement at the outset of the exchange is rejected. That

Aldöbern is being intractable in the face of Sylvester's attempts to control the situation is borne out instantly as he discharges his mission standing, accusing Sylvester of murder, and relaying, in the exact words of Rupert, the declaration of war on Warwand. The accusation is an extreme complement to the refusal to sit down; Sylvester has absolutely no control over the situation; stunned and disoriented by this sudden reversal, he remains weakly fixed on the chair as a focal point for his sense of order which is being assaulted by Aldöbern: "Ja so -- Nun setz dich, guter Freund"(595).[1]

On the linguistic level, Sylvester's battle continues; he attempts a verbal feint: "Sag an, ich habs vergessen, wo, wo bist du her?"(598-9) He hopes there is some mistake that will negate the declaration of Aldöbern. There is none, of course, but Aldöbern's answer, "Gebürtig? Herr, aus Oppenheim"(599), at least gives Sylvester a small wedge with which he attempts to dislodge the herald from his position of power -- a power, incidentally, of which Aldöbern is largely unaware -- and disarm the devastating accusation. It is a tangent off the real situation that seeks to incorporate Aldöbern into his world, in an entirely different way than in reality exists: "So, aus Oppenheim -- nun also aus Rossitz nicht. Ich wußt es wohl, nun setz dich"(600-1). He is thus not only trying to change simply the subject but also to alter the meaning of Aldöbern in the world, in Sylvester's beleaguered world upon which his consciousness and identity depend.

34

His last attempt to save his world by saving the surface is a plea to Aldöbern to give in and accept an artificial reality:

> Hat dir einer Unrecht,
> Beschimpfung, oder sonst was zugefügt,
> So sag dus mir, sags mir, wir wollens rächen. (607-9,
> emphasis mine)

Finally, Sylvester reaches the point where he is nearly begging Aldöbern to collude in the creation of a fiction. One can compare this aspect of the scene with Rupert's pleading with Santing to fabricate a legend about why Rupert had to kill Agnes:

> Santing!
> Warum denn hätt ich sie gemordet? Sage
> Mir schnell, ich bitte dich, womit sie mich
> Beleidigt, sags recht hämisch ... sprich, und weißt
> Du nichts, so lüg es! (2523-28)

Sylvester cannot counter the herald's accusation with an alternative state of affairs, or at least his attempts are unsuccessful.

At no time in this scene does Sylvester ask about the evidence, the real basis for Aldöbern's alleging that Sylvester is implicated in the murder of Peter. Sylvester tries to counter the mere verbal presentation of the threat on a verbal level himself. In essence, he accepts the accusation as real simply because it is expressed. The battle is for the dominance of one verbal construct over all others.[2] Words are the surface glue which holds the world together. There is a strange sense of obliqueness in this scene. One can scarcely describe this transaction as confrontation, argument, or conversation. Sylvester's evasion of Aldöbern's accusation -- the avoidance of confrontation -- is the dynamic, and words are both the threat and the defense. Aldöbern has the far easier job of it, of course; Sylvester comes up with many alternatives and suggestions. Aldöbern merely has to say no to all of them, repeat himself, and the accusation he has made stands intact. Sylvester's defensive manipulations result only in his own verbal and existential displacement. Sylvester's world crumbles with the word, and his identity crumbles with the content of his world.[3]

Transformation of identity in Kleist's characters often occurs, as it does in Sylvester, from such a base of linguistic operatives which expose and create anew the fibre of experiential knowledge. Verbal and existential realities become interdependent, each both a tool for manipulation as well as an expression of the changing status of self.

Chapter 4

NAMING AND KNOWLEDGE: THE REDUCTION OF PHENOMENA

Another linguistic model for controlling the flow of reality by
controlling the word is the process of creative naming which
permeates Kleist's texts. Characters frequently manipulate and,
indeed, create and defend their world through the ordering
linguistic activity of naming things, events, and people. The
name fixes reality in a static system which becomes the ground of
meaning and order for the individual. Though the things, systems,
and people may exist only verbally, they exist concretely for the
character. Once again, what in fact is real seems to be of less
importance in many cases than the capacity of the word to create
what it states, to create a person's world.

In the essay, "Über die Allmähliche Verfertigung der Gedanken
beim Reden," Kleist provides several examples of the motion
towards knowledge while speaking. Through his examples, this process reveals itself to be not so much a plowing through the vis-
cous medium of language to express a thought as an associative
maneuvering within the horizons of an individual's world until a
reality has become fixed: "so prägt ... das Gemüt, während die
Rede fortschreitet, ... jene verworrene Vorstellung zur völligen
Deutlichkeit aus, dergestalt, daß die Erkenntnis ... mit der

Periode fertig ist"(319-20). Contrasting this process with
meditation, Kleist tries to show that language itself is a mode of
consciousness, one form of knowledge rather than a mere representation of knowledge. One comes to know through expression.
Further, Kleist states in the essay: "Denn nicht _wir_ wissen, es
ist allererst ein gewisser _Zustand_ unsrer, welcher weiß"(323).
Kleist's choice of words is enlightening here as was the word
Erkenntnis in the previous citation. Kleist avoids fixing a
subject-object dichotomy, opposing reality with a fixed and
unchangeable subject which can "know" or "not know." The _Zustand_
of which he speaks represents the horizons of possible meanings,
the world of an individual, in all of his or her contexts. The
interdependence of identity, word, and world is once again
implied.

However, while the essay seems somewhat sanguine about the
possibility of an individual's coming to knowledge -- a more
complete knowledge -- through dialectic discourse with another
person in order to see from more than one perspective, this
process is not at all certain to occur in Kleist's creative works.
It is one of the most difficult things for his characters to do.
Characters seem engaged in a _private_ struggle to order and thus to
"know" their worlds, rather than in a social progression to a
shared world through discourse. The naming of phenomena is a
grasping and handling of aspects of reality, literally a verbal
manipulation of phenomena which reduces them to the "knowable,"
even though truth may not be approached in the process.

Let us consider several examples of this naming. Rupert's harangue, to which we referred above, is a relatively clear demonstration of the gradual forming of a knowledge of reality that is true only in relation to the speaker. Reality is simplified and fixed verbally, altered linguistically on the figurative plane. In the best demagogic manner, he proceeds to whip Rossitz into a vengeful frenzy of hate and aggression. The speech is amazing for its associative progression of thought and shift in perspective, for its crescendo of emotion and its peculiar style:

> Ich biete
> Euch, meine Lehensmänner, auf, mir schnell
> Von Mann und Weib und Kind, und was nur irgend
> Sein Leben lieb hat, eine Schar zu bilden.
> Denn nicht ein ehrlich offner Krieg, ich denke,
> Nur eine Jagd wirds werden, wie nach Schlangen.
> Wir wollen bloß das Felsenloch verkeilen,
> Mit Dampfe sie in ihrem Nest ersticken,
> --Die Leichen liegen lassen, daß von fernher
> Gestank die Gattung schreckt, und keine wieder
> In einem Erdenalter dort ein Ei legt. (64-73)

As in the process described in Kleist's essay, Rupert certainly is developing his thoughts through formulating them, but completion would hardly be an applicable term here since his perspective narrows rather than broadens. He proceeds associatively in his speech, moving from the real, the planned, the orderly, the purposeful, to the frightening vision of pitiless destruction. The associative, rather than logical, progression is revealed clearly by the paratactic and fragmentary style in his piling up of images. Kleist's use of anacoluthon here, a very frequent figure in the speech of his characters in other works as well, formally reveals the associative progression of Rupert's thought and formulation. He explosively launches himself away from the actual reality of the feud with Warwand, and the reality he is verbally creating threatens to overcome any contact with reality Rupert has when he begins the speech. He has not, unlike the model posited in the essay, entered into discourse with anything outside himself. There is, rather, a cyclic dynamic working here, that shows the words emanating from his private world which takes on new content as the words are integrated back into his world. In steps, a new world is created and molded, a world so complete and exclusive that he himself becomes lost in it. Eustache, frightened by this explosive departure from a shared world, tries to halt the spiral: "O Rupert, mäßge dich"(74). As Robert Labhardt and others have argued when discussing the use of language in Kleist's worlds, words do not merely reveal Rupert's world here, they help create it through naming.[1]

The metaphorical vision he verbalizes becomes concrete and, as propaganda, serves the function of reducing the enemy to something less than human, something repulsive, something one may destroy without compunction. Rupert removes the human dimension of his enemies through this naming of them as animals. The effect of this obviously goes further, of course, for he also removes any moral dimension from destroying his enemies, while retaining a positive moral quality for the community of Rossitz. But also, what began as a rhetorical manipulation of his audience -- and he does indeed gain control of the crowd which listens to him --

becomes something quite different as he loses himself along with them in his own creation.

It is particularly common in the play that the characters use various rhetorical devices to place others in categories that will capture their "essence" and to reduce the essence of adversaries to a word which will define them as pure evil. There is a kind of equation between epistemological and ontological issues here, as if the "knowing" of others somehow neutralizes the effectiveness of that person and his acts. As Rupert says at one point, still thinking in terms of the animal metaphors he had created earlier: "O listig ist die Schlange -- 's ist nur gut, daß wir das wissen, denn so ist sies nicht für uns"(1542-4, emphasis Kleist's). The knowing and naming is a creation of order and of a kind of subjective certainty and safety; control is retained, or so the speaker may believe. Ottokar handily reduces Jeronimus to the uncomplicated status of simply being an enemy:

> Und weils jetzt drängt, und eben nicht die Zeit,
> Zu mäkeln, ein zweideutig Körnchen Saft
> Mit Müh herauszuklauben, nun so machen
> Wirs kurz, und sagen: du gehörst zu Warwand. (131-4,
>   emphasis mine)

With that final linguistic dispatch of the person of Jeronimus there is no desire or need to speak further of the matter. It is sufficient: "wir hätten, denk ich, nun einander wohl nichts mehr zu sagen?"(156-7) Jeronimus in turn deals with Sylvester in the same way later: "Doch nicht so vielen Atem bist du wert, als nur dies einzge Wort mir kostet: Schurke!"(679-80) In these cases the character stops all motion in the environment, halts time, and freezes reality into a static formulation that, for the reader, has reality only in its formulation. For the character who tampers with the complexity of his or her environment in this way, however, the simplification provides an unambiguous setting in which accurate and direct action may be taken. Characters remove others from the complexity of context.

In "Die Verlobung in St. Domingo," just as in Schroffenstein, there is a tendency, indeed, a compulsive need, to simplify the complexities of fluid reality and reduce characters and phenomena by fixing them linguistically. Congo Hoango has a fixed word for whites -- "diese weißen Hunde, wie er sie nannte"(161).[2] Like Rupert's animalization of his enemies, this is a reduction which presses any dimension of humanity out of them together with any claim to respect. This simplification continues throughout the novella. When Toni seeks to give the appearance of solidarity with the revolutionary force, she demonstrates her "correct thought" similarly by placing individuals in simplified categories; she speaks to Babekan of the whites, referring to "die ganze Unmenschlichkeit der Gattung zu der dieser Fremde <gehört>"(179, emphasis mine).[3] This imposition of a simplified linguistic reality on a complex and highly differentiated structure of worlds is really a jargon which reveals and creates a pattern of prejudiced thought and belief. It works, of course, remarkably well in this novella which deals so much with the shallow mind-sets of both black and white prejudice. Manifestations of individuality are insignificant and impotent in the face of this overpowering model of reality which reduces everything to, literally, black and white, a model which defines others and also serves as the sole means of self-definition as well. The model is unassailable by virtue of its very simplicity which excludes any outside considerations that might invalidate it.

The "Verlobung" is a story in good measure precisely about the simplification of reality and the loss of humanity stemming from a reduction in the complexity of the characters' experiencing of reality. The model of creative naming is clearly a defensive use of language in the instances we have discussed so far. Underlying these situations is a fear within the characters that control must be established over what is happening to them. If the environment -- and this means above all one's fellow man in Kleist's works -- can be named, it becomes known and thus more manageable. Beneath this fear is the feeling that somehow the environment is not theirs, and they attempt to make it theirs, to possess it, through language.

Linguistic fixation of individuals and phenomena is not only a means to define threats in the environment. It is also a means of removing them from one's world. Like the defining of others as one's enemies, pockets of safety are verbally created in the environment by characters who proclaim other key individuals to be reliable, trustworthy, like-minded. This represents a wish by the speaker that can become more real than reality. Gustav, for example, in his insecurity and fear and desperate desire for a sympathetic soul, even a savior, manufactures just such a person in Toni. We note the remarkably short time in which he develops a trust in her. At a turning point in the novella the narrator tells us, "Der Fremde ... _nannte_ sie sein liebes Mädchen, und

schloß sie, wie durch göttliche Hand von jeder Sorge erlöst, in
seine Arme"(173, emphasis mine). That his creation of a bond
between them has, at this point at least, more effect on him and
more validity for him than for her or than the situation warrants,
is obvious but largely beside the point. It is exactly his
creation of a person who does not in fact exist that moves the
story forward. And of course we soon read that Gustav, after the
period of a few hours since seeing her for the first time, "nannte
sie ... seine liebe Braut," and pledges to her his eternal
love(176). Gustav's naming of her, a proclamation of knowledge
rather than a statement of truth, is his attempt to control his
world. Characters repeatedly decide they "know" things to be
true.

That Kleist wishes to emphasize the gap between what is real
and what is wished for, becomes clear when we later hear Gustav's
words again, this time out of Hoango's mouth. When Hoango makes
the decision that Toni is loyal to him, an assumption which is as
ill-founded in fact as was Gustav's original assumption, we hear
that Congo, too, "nannte sie sein liebes Mädchen"(186). In these
parallel situations which echo each other, both men are not simply
mistaken, nor are they simply projecting an emotion into the
substance of another person. They create a desired sentiment out
of their own need, fabricate the realization of that sentiment,
declare the reality of that vision, express knowledge of it, and,
on the basis of the product of that process, expect reciprocity of
the sentiment from another person and fulfillment of the vision.
The fact that they use the possessive adjective -- mein liebes

Mädchen -- rather than the indefinite article, is not simply the attachment of the overt expression of the desired bond and loyalty; rather, this linguistic grasping further suggests to us the possessiveness and the personal, creative, private nature of the construct.

The parallel in Schroffenstein is Johann's creation of a savior in Agnes:

> Möge
> Die Ähnliche der Mutter Gottes auch
> Maria heißen -- uns nur, du verstehst. (319-21).

He and Ottokar christen her Maria; she becomes a private reality to which access can be gained through the code word, "Maria." Gustav's creations as a motor for the story are not matched by Johann's, of course, since the latter's insanity renders him simply anti-social and nearly completely solipsistic, and our interest in him as a subject in the story is lessened considerably. Ottokar carries on the construct of a Maria, however, and the possessive aspects of his creation are obvious. Even after Ottokar and Agnes have in theory come to understand and trust each other -- have come to share a world, in other words -- it is his world which for him must be the controlling one in possession of all validity of experience. "Kann ich dich ganz mein nennen?" he asks with the same self-referential defensiveness that Gustav displays. Agnes is quite accurate in her irked reply: "Denn nicht wirst du verlangen, daß ich mit deinen Augen sehen soll" (1359-60).

This possessiveness is a foreshadowing of the possessive love which proves to be so disastrous in Penthesilea precisely because it does not emanate from or move towards a shared world. In the fifteenth scene of the play -- the "recognition" scene -- it becomes obvious that Penthesilea seeks the legend of Achilles, the construct about the man, rather than the complex human being. Indeed, Achilles also needs a name for the object of his desiring and he repeatedly asks who she is(1774, 1811, 1812-13).[4] But it is Penthesilea who demonstrates the possessiveness to a dehumanizing degree. At first she scrutinizes him and doubts it is he, that is, doubts he is his legend, for she finds his appearance too soft and mild to tally with the reports of what he is as a semi-divine hero(1790). It is upon Prothoe's assurance, citing the forging of his armor by Thetis, that Penthesilea accepts his identity, as Achilles but not as an individual.

On first encounter, the way she addresses him becomes a taking possession of him:

> Nun denn, so grüß ich dich mit diesem Kuß,
> Unbändigster der Menschen, mein! Ich bins,
> Du junger Kriegsgott, der du angehörst;
> Wenn man im Volk dich fragt, so nennst du mich. (1805-8,
>   emphasis Kleist's)

His existence is not independent of her experience. A mutual confirmation of legend and experience occurs for her, none of it outside her experiencing of him as construct. It is only after his death, when in fact he is a shredded corpse, that her tone changes noticeably, and she takes note of him in a warm personal way, twice calling him "this youth"(2929, 3013), and "beloved," a nomenclature which apprehends him for the first time as an individual with his own world, ironically when he is no longer a person.[5]

This is identical to the naming activity, for names, too, lose the basic Cartesian or Lockean function of discrimination, the distinction of one phenomenon from another. The name grants phenomena meaning that may be independent of the phenomena themselves. Kleist underscores this dimension by suggesting that language used in this fashion can have a near religious quality, and is a most peculiar kind of knowledge and seeing. Certainly Penthesilea's kiss and taking possession of Achilles has a ritualistic tone about it, as obviously does Johann's and Ottokar's ceremonial "baptism" of Maria *in absentia*, but the ceremonial aspect of this ordering of the environment -- specifically of other people -- is nowhere more apparent than in Gustav's naming of Toni. The creation in Toni of a pocket of safety within the revolution-torn country goes beyond his earlier decision that she is a sympathetic soul. His consciousness alters her with a complete ceremonial transformation of her identity into that of Mariane Congreve, his late betrothed. This transformation is a transformation of his consciousness, of course, not a transformation of Toni, but at issue here is the ordering of reality for the subject and the creating of phenomena for the knower.

Seeking a refuge, Gustav creates it in Toni, and the process demonstrates the interrelationship among various forms of knowing. First, Gustav notices "eine entfernte Ähnlichkeit" between Toni and someone else -- "er wußte noch selbst nicht recht mit wem"(172). And after he has discovered -- or, more accurately, decided -- that Toni is not a threat to him, he is struck by what has become for him "eine wunderbare Ähnlichkeit" between Toni and Mariane(173). Quite clearly his visual perception is not the source of this change; it is not a question of a _Versehen_. She is beginning to change, through his experience of her. Toni has in fact helped to trigger this sequence of events, for when sitting on Gustav's lap she plays briefly with the cross around his neck. When she does this his memory seems to be activated. It is immediately after this that he begins to believe that he is safe. Gustav retells the story of Mariane's death, and her death in his memory and in the retelling has attained the significance of Christ's sacrificial death. We have no check on the nature of Mariane as an individual other than the legend which Gustav creates in his recall of past events, but he experiences her in recall in a different way than as a complex person, something he is about to do with Toni as well.[6] Mariane in her essence and naming is an _ideal_ of salvation for him, reduced nearly completely to a tableau of her one gesture of love and sacrifice, dying for his "crime," dying that he might live: "'Sie starb,' antwortete der Fremde, 'und ich lernte den Inbegriff aller Güte und Vortrefflichkeit erst mit ihrem Tode kennen'"(174). The stabilization and fixation of Mariane, of her meaning for him, apparent in the religious overtones of his retelling, is a reflection of the stabilization and fixation of her in his memory.[7]

Two separate modes of consciousness, memory and verbal expression, confirm each other because they really represent the same activity -- a conscious "knowing" of Mariane. They are played off against other modes of consciousness -- perception and anticipation -- in order to complete this process. In short, the role with which he is about to christen Toni is itself a construct of consciousness, a creative knowing that bypasses other possible orderings of reality and bypasses the complexity of Mariane as a woman in favor of her as a concept, a battery of knowledge that is "his" Mariane.

It is after the relation of the story of Mariane to Toni that a peculiar ceremony takes place. After making love to Toni, Gustav sees that he has been saved -- "gerettet," he says, just as he had been saved by Mariane.[8] That he repeatedly uses the perfect tense when thinking of himself as safe after gaining control of Toni, reveals a premature sense of security, to say the least; he is still well embedded in a perilous situation for many reasons. The sexual possession of her is definitely the turning point in his view of his situation; he becomes less able to see the lurking dangers because he has removed the threats in his own mind. Now, just as he earlier named Toni "sein liebes Mädchen," as if by naming her, her essence became "known" to him, so he now removes from his neck what had been a gift from Mariane, a golden cross, and gives it to Toni -- "ein Brautgeschenk, wie er es nannte"(175). · The flavor of this scene is ritualistic: he caresses her, bows over her, hangs the cross about her neck, and soon we hear again, "<er> nannte sie noch einmal seine liebe Braut"(176). The ritual solemnizes not only a betrothal. It is the placing of the role of Mariane upon Toni; it is a ritual of change from Toni to Mariane. With the bestowal of the signal

accoutrements of that role of selfless love, of devotion, of
redeeming sacrifice, he transforms her into Mariane for himself.

It is not so much a display of trust as the creation of an
agent who is worthy of trust. It is an active modification of
reality that incorporates Toni into his world, but certainly not
as Toni. In his attempts to find safety, he evades reality
through the very control he tries to exert over reality. The
betrothal ceremony's religious dimension has less to do with the
betrothal itself than with the magical power of his transforming
of the world. The social dimension that one assumes to be present
in a betrothal ceremony is hardly apparent, for no dialogue occurs
in the scene. The communication is not a discourse but a
communing over and in his reconstructed vision of Mariane; even
the communing is thus artificial, a facade built upon a facade.

Further, it becomes clear that although he incorporates Toni
into his world through this betrothal, it is not as Toni. He is
locked into his illusion of her as a white. He has, in his mind,
never lost his desire to return to the sanctuary of the white
world, and this is clear on the symbolic level of the novella.
While he gives Toni Mariane's cross, an obvious symbol of
salvation, he sends his ring to Strömli the next day. This
gesture is, in the story, a way to demonstrate that the messenger
boy Nanky is indeed a messenger from Gustav, but it is also a sign
that Gustav is "wedded" to his white world. He never really
enters any portion of Toni's world.

Chapter 5

THE CONTROL OF TRUTH

In the examples discussed in the preceding sections, the manipulation of words by Kleist's characters really represents the
manipulation of phenomena and experience. Even when more than one
person is involved, the scene is usually not a dialogue, for one
partner is not a participant in the game and is not actually
viewed by the other as a real person. Only the activity of one
subject initially determines the content of the process. It is
this dehumanizing reification of another subject, a thinking away
of another's subjectivity, which underlies the frequent toying
with others that is such a hallmark of the interpersonal
relationships in most of Kleist's texts. The creation of what
one's partners are is a destructive sort of relationship which
frequently prevents a genuine encounter between individuals -- in
friendship, in love, or in sex.

There is obviously a lack of honesty in this manner of
knowing and existing, a dishonesty in the way characters deal with
themselves, with others, with the world. Enmeshed in myriad fears
and needs, the characters create meaning not out of what actually
exists, but out of what exists for them -- or what they want to be
true. In addition to the models of manipulating presentation and

of naming, word-dreams or wishes are also a means of attempting to control what is true. They are fundamentally related to the other manipulative word games that we have discussed. The playing of these games is always serious, for the import of these games goes beyond knowing to the creation of one's world and to one's entire relationship with the world. The choice of such terms as "game" and "play" is not fortuitous here, for the basic nature of play is related to this manipulative mental activity. One essential aspect of play -- and here one can build on Huizinga's discussion in Homo Ludens and arrive at some contrastive insights -- is the suspension of our normal world.[1] In play, a suspension of the rules of normal reality occurs: in make-believe games things may "just happen," and even in formalized games where new and different rules are put into force, a suspension of the binding strictures of time and space and causality occurs.

What becomes apparent instantly is that for Kleist's characters, this play activity does not have as its purpose a relaxation from the rules of our usual world, as is the case with Huizinga's description of play in culture. For Kleist's characters this manipulation of the rules of reality and this creation of artificial realities have existential import. The games are, in fact, a way of being for the characters and a way in which a world comes into being for the characters. We have seen that others and the world may exist only as fictions, created by a character. The question of dishonesty comes into the discussion not because the world of the characters does not coincide with reality -- the dependence of the world on the subject is the underlying premise and necessary mechanism of the ground rules of knowing in Kleist's experimental worlds. Rather, this dishonesty arises when phenomena are tampered with and altered by consciousness and when the subject closes his or her self off from reality in manipulative activity. Remaining for the moment within the framework of the characters as game-players in Kleist's works, one can see that the activity of knowing in the instances we are now discussing is characterized by self-delusion.[2]

The linguistic model of the wish -- or word-dream, if one prefers -- shows the characters' attempts to control the flow of reality as do the other models discussed above. A wish may be a simple thing, but since the words in Kleist's works are frequently tantamount to reality itself, the significance of a wish for Kleist's characters can make wishing very different from mere idle fantasizing about what might be. Kleist's characters are unlikely to utter a statement to the effect that they wish something were true, because they tend simply to use the power of the word to create what it states. But the process may be quite visible nonetheless, as it is, for example, in _Amphitryon_. Alkmene, in act II, scene 5, is speaking with Jupiter. Like the confrontation between Sylvester and Aldöbern, it is a battle to see which of the two verbal systems used by the participants will be victorious. Jupiter throws out questions and hypothetical realities -- what if Amphitryon were Jupiter and Jupiter Amphitryon. Alkmene is put in the position of having to respond to these verbal constructs; she must fight words with words. She does quite well in this scene, bandying about and weaving formulations that prevent Jupiter from

effectively penetrating her own verbal defenses and from forcing
her to confront the awful problem she in fact does face.

The final question, what would she do if he, whom she deems
to be Amphitryon, were Jupiter and at that very moment Amphitryon
should appear, is irreducible and seemingly offers no way out.
She seems to be forced to confront that reality which -- even in
the contemplation, as it later is shown -- would threaten to
unhinge her. She does manage to evade this threat with relative
ease, however, by constructing in effect a wish of a wish:

> Wenn du, der Gott, mich hier umschlungen hieltest
> Und jetzo sich Amphitryon mir zeigte,
> Ja -- dann traurig würde ich sein, und wünschen,
> Daß er der Gott mir wäre, und daß du
> Amphitryon mir bliebst, wie du es bist. (1564-8)

The first two lines of her response are a verbatim repetition of
Jupiter's position of the hypothetical reality, and they do not
represent an actual internalization or even recognition of the
problem. Her actual reaction follows the "ja." The wish would be
simply to alter that situation presented, by altering what she
experiences. The second level of this evasion of the problem is
the verbal construction of the wish itself and the resulting
evasion of the interrogation situation she is in. Ultimately, the
threat from either the hypothetical or the real confrontation with
an Amphitryon and a non-Amphitryon is to her unity of self, her
identity, but this disaster would be caused by the destruction of
her cognitive control. It is that structure of control of her
experience that she is defending and asserting, not the truth. In
this scene, at least, her verbal playing is as removed from

reality as was Sosias' posing which we noted at the outset of the play.

Word play, however, need not be so directly stated to be a wish; the process is not always so clearly announced. Virtually all of the models discussed thus far are types of word-dreams, fictions created outside the real environment. Characters transport themselves to new worlds by transforming their experience of the environment. The statement of reality is sufficient means to accomplish this. The term "word-dream" is appropriate here, because a dream _per se_ is a mode of consciousness that need not be verbalized in order to be lived. But when created for or with another person, the fiction becomes a word-dream, meant to be expressed in order to be shared. The love between Toni and Gustav is built upon a shared vision of selfless love which is accepted as a platform and framework for their own love. These individuals, in order to find refuge and to experience happiness and fulfillment amid the dangers of the starkly reduced, black and white environment which was described above, create a private world and a common vision through reveries of a better world, through fantasies of a future which is a place for individuals to meet and love, and through memories of better times and places. Unlike Jeronimo and Josephe in the "Erdbeben," who are formulating plans for the future after being released from real threats, temporarily at least, Toni and Gustav have nothing outside themselves that significantly supports their fantasy. When Gustav and Toni are together, and when they think of each other, they freeze the compelling flux of the world around them, and slip out of time and space. Toni absorbs and lives in Gustav's description of their future home -- with its fields, garden, meadows, vineyards, and a loving and grateful father(175); and she dreams of the time when -- "als sein treues Weib" -- she can travel to Europe, that _fata morgana_ for her, and can open her soul completely to Gustav(183).

Gustav, as well, achieves comfort when he retreats to that vision, and he also slips into the memory of the halcyon days of youth and the memory of the love of Mariane. When he sleeps, he dreams and exists in that better world with Toni. They build on and reinforce each other's vision, colluding in the creation of a private world which is posited by Gustav, and they spend a great deal of time in this private world. The stuff of dreaming is preceded by the word. The private world, especially for Gustav, becomes the seat of his existence, and Toni, the more realistic of the two, clearly recognizes the greater need for Gustav to exist outside of the environment. We are told at one point that Toni is reluctant to wake the dreaming Gustav: "sie konnte sich nicht entschließen, ihn aus den Himmeln lieblicher Einbildung in die Tiefe einer gemeinen und elenden Wirklichkeit herabzureißen"(184).

This attempt to draw another into one's private world is made frequently in the texts, a sort of "let me take you away from all this" device that seeks collusion in and confirmation of one's own experience. Like Gustav's and Toni's private world, the world into which Graf F. tries to woo the Marquise von O... in the garden scene is an artificial and dreamt reality. He approaches her in the garden of the estate which has become the limit of her

world of retreat. Cast out from her family and from society --
unjustly, she knows --, she is forced to establish herself in
this, her private world, a redoubt of unknown innocence and
unbelieved truth. Practically, it is a private world that
signifies withdrawal from reality and contains only herself and
the unquestioning presence of her children. The Graf in essence
comes and offers her his trusting knowledge of her as a
replacement for the world she has lost; he comes to her, he says,
in spite of the world, in spite of her family, and even in spite
of her pregnancy. What marks his overture to her is that he seems
to be presenting her with a way out of her retreat, but this is
true in only a limited fashion. His desire to save her, though
clearly genuine by this time, is inextricably bound up with his
desire to save himself, and here his problem lies. At this point
in the story it is still not emotionally or practically possible
for him to reveal his dreadful secret, neither to Julietta nor to
the world. It is Julietta who later paves the way for both of
them to reintegrate themselves into society. What he suggests at
this moment in Julietta's walled-in garden, however, is that they
can live alone, in their love for each other. He states he will
ignore the world's opinion of Julietta, and he does so -- not only
for her sake, but for his own as well. It is a sort of collusion
that he requests in this scene, a collusion that has elements of
self-deception in it.

Not all word-dreams which Kleist's characters create are
necessarily a means of self-delusion, of course. The word-dream
which Ottokar creates for the sake of Agnes -- "mit einem

plötzlich heitern Spiel" -- at the end of <u>Schroffenstein</u>, hides impending danger from her, transporting her through a fable set in a future they never live to see: the description of their wedding, the union of the two families, and their wedding night(2410). Delivered in the present tense, this verbal reality is fabricated to shield her by replacing the real and definitely inescapable predicament in which they are. She does move into it briefly, both emotionally and physically when Ottokar describes their wedding night and she allows him to undress her. The action thus has two different meanings, because it is experienced in two different worlds: for her, displaced in space and time to an artificial world of the wedding night, and for him in the concrete situation as he tries to disguise himself with her clothes. It is this multiplicity of meanings which betokens the relativity of reality in the sense that reality has meaning only in relation to a given subject. The much heralded misunderstandings which flesh out the dialogues in Kleist's works have their origin in this fact and at times also in the evasion of reality by the participants in a dialogue.[3] Language itself does not cause the misunderstanding by an inherent lack of validity.

Ottokar and Agnes in this scene present an unusual case, in a way. His deception of Agnes does not come from a defense of himself. Unlike the Graf's approach to Julietta in the garden, which demonstrates that he is in part deluding himself, Ottokar's motivation is oriented entirely towards Agnes: his interest is in Agnes, and he is literally giving up his self to save her. Ottokar could not escape in any case, nor could Agnes. The disguises they adopt fail because each disguise has its own mortal enemy, regardless of who is beneath the disguise: the false reality they create in the entire love grotto scene is not capable of existence.

It is worth drawing attention to the fact that Ottokar and Agnes share -- or rather, develop -- an interrelationship that is truly open. They do come to share a world by releasing their defensive grasp on their own individual worlds somewhat and opening their selves to the other person. This is unusual in Kleist's works, and it is marked by what is one of the very rare instances of shared irony in Kleist's works. In the recognition scene, act III, scene 1, Ottokar and Agnes open themselves to each other and express their love after the climactic episode when Agnes thought Ottokar was poisoning her. As they tenderly take leave of each other, Ottokar initiates a brief exchange:

```
OTTOKAR                          Nun gut;
   Das nächstemal geb ich dir Gift.
AGNES lacht                          Frisch aus
   Der Quelle, du trinkst mit. (1496-8)
```

Ottokar laughs likewise. This is word play, too; a hypothetical situation is posited. But the elusive activity is entirely missing here in a joke, a shared irony. Considering the linguistic usage by characters elsewhere in Kleist's works, it is surprising indeed to have someone say and create something that is not true, indeed, is the opposite of what is true, know that it is neither real nor true, anticipate and know that the other will share that, and to have the receiver of the words in fact know as well that what was said was neither real nor true. It seems the most unlikely and the most difficult of occurrences.

To open the self to such a degree is very hard for Kleist's characters in any case. Ottokar and Agnes achieve, at least subjectively, a level of knowledge and control over reality because they see -- at that moment, at least -- that they have no need to evade reality to defend themselves. They already feel in control and set out hopefully to enlighten others. For most of Kleist's characters, who by their nature already desperately defend their private worlds and the structure of self, it is made all the more difficult because of the threats of the exceedingly nasty environments and situations into which Kleist places his characters in order to test them and their responses. That sort of existential relaxation is beyond them.

Concluding our discussion of models for controlling the flow of reality are the two models which are basically corollaries of the aspects we have already treated. The elusion of reality by preventing its verbal expression and, second, by the fleeing to the metaphorical realm, are models related to the creative naming activity of consciousness. What is _not_ said may be the denial of a particular reality, a creative removal of some aspect of the environment. The Marquise's mother, for example, at the end of the novella, renders the Graf's nefarious act the deed that never was by cutting off further recognition of the matter through the ceremonial pronouncement, "so sind wir alle versöhnt, so ist alles vergeben und vergessen"(141). The conscious "forgetting" is the obliteration of a rather unforgettable sequence of events and not merely a cliche. In the same novella, this sort of denial of reality appears repeatedly. In the scene where the resurrected Graf appears and proposes to Julietta, the increasingly uncomfortable Commandant combats the assault on the order of his house not only with the gestures we discussed above, but also by using silence to combat these stresses as if they would cease to exist if they remained unexpressed. When the Graf persists in demanding an answer to his proposal, he requests the Graf "von dieser Sache abzubrechen," and he tries to literally change the subject of conversation(112). We then hear of the Commandant: "<er> forderte die Familie auf, davon weiter nicht in seiner Gegenwart zu sprechen"(115). And to his wife and son he later forbids any mention of his daughter after he has ordered her to remove herself:

> Der Kommandant bat immer auf eine Art, die einem Befehle
> gleich sah, zu schweigen; versicherte, ... daß er sein
> Gedächtnis ihrer ganz zu vertilgen wünsche; und meinte,
> er hätte keine Tochter mehr. (131)[4]

While saying this he also removes a portrait of her, the remaining phenomenal evidence of his daughter's existence. It is as if he believed that if he removed his consciousness of an object -- Julietta -- then the object of his consciousness would be destroyed. He attempts to cleanse various modes of consciousness -- memory, and, by implication, anticipation, the perceptual modes of hearing and sight, language. The past, present, and future are thus reordered. The same process is visible in Robert Guiskard, the hero of which attempts to deny the plague's invasion of his body by controlling the very mention of the possibility. He interrupts the old man's query as to why he has not been quite fit the last few days: " 's ist der Red nicht wert, sag ich!"(460) The vehemence of his denial clearly suggests the degree to which the importance of the denial touches his existence. Kleist fills a subsequent line with poetic irony; Guiskard proclaims to the assembled masses: "Seit wann denn gilt mein Guiskardwort nicht mehr?"(576) The Guiskard-word is indeed an attempt to destroy the indestructable.[5]

In "Die Marquise von O...," Julietta's mother makes a joke which is of a very different ilk than the joke of Ottokar and Agnes, illustrating a closed rather than an open self. In the earlier part of the novella, in particular, the communications among the family members do not appear to be abundant or personal in nature at any point. There is a suggestion of privacy about their interactions, a suggestion that none of the family really reveals personal problems or causes any disturbance in the harmonious and problem-free domestic idyll that they believe exists and in which disturbances are sidestepped. The Marquise suffers, for example, "ganze Wochen lang" from nausea, dizziness, and fainting; yet there is no indication that she communicates this illness, which, in someone otherwise so healthy, must be alarming. In the first domestic scene we witness in the story, a scene immediately following the narrator's account of the Marquise's symptoms, the family is sitting at tea, but there is no impression of any conversation taking place or having taken place. Indeed, after the Commandant leaves, the Marquise wakens "aus einer langen Gedankenlosigkeit"(109). Her relation to her mother

of the strange sensation of feeling as if she were pregnant
provokes an odd response; her mother makes light of it: "Frau von
G... sagte, sie würde vielleicht den Phantasus gebären, und
lachte." The Marquise, whose comment was not meant to be
laughable, takes her cue from her mother and jokes likewise:
"Morpheus wenigstens, versetzte die Marquise, oder einer der
Träume aus seinem Gefolge, würde sein Vater sein, und scherzte
gleichfalls." The Commandant returns and nothing more is said of
the matter, nor is the subject broached again until the actual
revelation of pregnancy destroys the order in the family.

This scene is striking because of what fails to be said and
what is not permitted to be said in this, the most discursive and
conversational of Kleist's novellas. If such a scene appeared in
Jane Austen's prose, for example, a conversational gambit such as
the Marquise's on the subject of her health and such a strange
sensation, would at once have become the subject of the most
earnest and concerned debate and cause for distressed empathy.
Here it is tersely dismissed and forgotten. While one would not
expect such an expansive discussion in a novella as in an Austen
novel, the silence and the joking reaction of the Marquise's
mother is significant, because it prevents the reality of a
concrete personal problem, her daughter's health, from being
discussed by removing the problem to a sphere of fantasy and by
disarming the Marquise's utterance of its substance through humor.
It is not callousness at work here but rather a tendency to avoid
any disruption of the cool order which obtains in the household.[6]

Metaphors and analogies frequently function in a very similar manner of evasion and the defense of order in the individual's world. Unlike some conceptions of the metaphor which are based on a shared similarity between two phenomena, metaphors, similes, and analogies are at times used by characters in Kleist's texts to remove a phenomenon from reality to a different plane, which alters the meaning of the phenomenon. A metaphor of this sort should not be viewed as some type of connection to some noumenal truth, nor should it be viewed as the expression of the soul, which bypasses the everyday language of communication.[7]

The metaphorical plane is unassailable and carries its own rules with it; it gains an independence from objective reality. In Schroffenstein it is a common means of argument and presentation of "facts." When Johann sees the budding relationship between Ottokar and Maria/Agnes, he skips over the actual concrete situation and expresses himself to Ottokar through analogy:

> Wenn einer mir vertraut', er wiss ein Roß,
> Das ihm bequem sei, und er kaufen wolle,
> Und ich, ich ginge heimlich hin und kaufts
> Mir selbst--was meinst du, wäre das wohl edel? (818-21)

On the plane of analogous presentation, the only possible answer Ottokar could give is no. It is not surprising that Ottokar refuses to argue on that plane: "Sehr schief wählst du dein Gleichnis"(822). Johann fails in his attempt to maneuver Ottokar into an admission of guilt, but any acceptance by Ottokar of the validity of the images which Johann presents would have led to a successful attempt to shift the relationships of reality. Ottokar, in the manner we have seen elsewhere, simply discards the words entirely.

Other characters in the drama use the metaphor to define their own situation or to rationalize their own action or inaction. Both Ottokar and Eustache, for example, abdicate their responsibility for their own acts and plead the impossibility of action in opposition to Rupert. Eustache says of herself, "doch muß die Flagge wehen, wohin der Wind"(1637-8). And Ottokar uses similar imagery: "Er trägt uns, wie die See das Schiff, wir müssen mit seiner Woge fort, sie ist nicht zu beschwören"(1453-5). They state a problem less than they create a figurative model that is convincing and indisputable because of its lack of direct relationship with reality and with the actual position of the characters in it. The images they choose are closed and in themselves correct, yet, removed from the flux of human context, they are unarguable because a counterstatement cannot counter the image on the figurative level, even though it might be possible if the basis of the description were on the real and human level alone. The metaphor actually takes over. For example, "sie" in Ottokar's speech refers in reality to Rupert, yet the pronoun gender has been fixed by the metaphor and never returns to the actual point of discussion even though Ottokar could have begun a new sentence there that would have related the metaphor directly to the explanation. Ottokar and Eustache are really talking to themselves here, convincing themselves that they cannot act, and justifying their lack of action.[8]

In this discussion we have chosen language because it is the most accessible mode of consciousness, but not because it is the only one. We have seen that knowledge precedes reality and that language is but one way of knowing. We might well have chosen as a starting point other possible modes of consciousness -- memory, dreaming, imagination, anticipation, perception, and trust -- to name modes which are highly visible in the mental activity of Kleist's characters. The modes are not interchangeable, but the very fact that different modes may be set against each other and may be replaced by others is one of the most illuminating observations we may make at the conclusion of our discussion. Characters move the totality of mind and with it their selves into different modes of consciousness, creating a diversity of interesting situations and problems. Problems which the characters face can be compounded by or even can emanate directly from this dis-integration of consciousness and from the characters' subjective movement into and out of their environment. It is not difficult to appreciate the frustration and sympathy of Prothoe, who exclaims to Penthesilea, for whom dreaming is virtually where she exists:

> Penthesilea! O du Träumerin!
> In welchen fernen Glanzgefilden schweift
> Dein Geist umher, mit unruhvollem Flattern,
> Als ob sein eigner Sitz ihm nicht gefiele,
> Indes das Glück, gleich einem jungen Fürsten,
> In deinen Busen einkehrt, und, verwundert
> Die liebliche Behausung leer zu finden,
> Sich wieder wendet und zum Himmlischen
> Die Schritte wieder flüchtig setzen will? (1538-46)

Penthesilea later, in another shift, is herself baffled by dream and reality becoming confused. Her real defeat at the hands of

Achilles is absorbed as a dream when she subsequently recalls it,
and when she sees real matrimonial roses, the discrepancy remotely
forces itself on her, and troubled, she strokes her forehead and
must exclaim, "Ach mein böser Traum!"(1719) Such elusions and
confusions are commonplace in the texts, and there is that
recurring element of mendacity in the way characters exist through
the setting of one mode of experience against another. Many of
Kleist's characters feel the compulsive and fearful need to
control the environment, or, failing that, to deny the existence
of threatening aspects of reality.

Control of the environment and the manipulation of the
objects of consciousness go hand in hand. The desire to control
is even readily apparent in the objective correlative of
manipulative experiencing -- the physical manipulation, the
grasping of phenomena. When we first see Agnes in Schroffenstein,
for example, she is engaged in arranging and ordering the natural
randomness of flowers into a wreath for a specifically human
reason: to create an aesthetic object of human perception
(719-23). And when Sylvester first appears, he is speaking of a
human design of nature, the ordering of the garden: "Ausreißen
ist ein froh Geschäft, geschieht's um etwas Besseres zu
pflanzen"(490-1).

His statement might well apply to the mental acrobatics of
the characters we have discussed in this chapter and others we
will examine later. Gustav, whose elusive thought we have viewed
from many sides, is marked by a parallel touching and controlling
and grasping of virtually everything around him, but especially of

people. He strokes, kisses, and seduces Toni -- and falls prey to the creation of his seduction. He grasps hands, holds hands, weeps on hands, embraces and encloses others in his arms, all tangible signs of his groping for solidity, physical manifestations of his attempt to control the people with whom he must deal in his frightening circumstances.[9] Inversely, the great fear is to lose control, even in a physical sense. This account, in which the action is carried as much by the gestures as by the words spoken, visually epitomizes Gustav's plight in the story:

> "Geschwind!" sprach <Toni>, indem sie seine Hand ergriff und ihn nach der Tür zog: "hier herein!" ... Wer bist du? rief der Fremde sträubend .... Wer wohnt in diesem Hause ...? "Niemand, bei dem Licht der Sonne," sprach das Mädchen, "als meine Mutter und ich!" und bestrebte und beeiferte sich, ihn mit sich fortzureißen. Was niemand! rief der Fremde, indem er, mit einem Schritt rückwärts, seine Hand losriß .... "Ich sage, nein!" sprach das Mädchen, indem sie ... mit dem Fuß stampfte .... Und damit zog sie den Fremden mit ihren beiden Händen in das Haus hinein ... ergriff, nachdem sie die Tür erreicht, des Fremden Hand und führte ihn die Treppe hinauf, nach dem Zimmer ihrer Mutter. (163)

The "environment" of these troubled characters should not be viewed merely as being composed of things, but rather it is the totality of everything that is not self. People, and words themselves, are phenomena which are assigned meaning by the mind in the quest for control. Further, the focus of these needs is always the self. Fictions and forms are desperately defended in the citadel of consciousness, as it is called in reference to the pressed Amphitryon. Space and time are halted, shifted, and fixed; the plane of reality can be bypassed; phenomena are created, destroyed, and tossed about -- all to create or retain frameworks and structures that will allow the maintenance and survival of the private worlds of the individual or allow survival itself.

The very activity of manipulation and defense marks the vulnerability of the self. The retention and fabrication of a surface of experience reveals the characters' longing to be saved somehow. Creatively, characters fabricate false heavens and non-existent others, idylls of safety, and an unreal "we" in worlds outside of space and time. We have seen it with Johann, Ottokar, and the Graf, with Gustav and Toni, and it is elsewhere, too, in Käthchen von Heilbronn's and Strahl's marriage and in Alkmene's desire to retreat to a stressless world: "Was brauchen wir, als nur uns selbst?" she asks. We shall further explore these fictions and the extent to which individuals confirm each other's fictions.

There is often a fear of life at work here, sometimes forced on characters willy-nilly, sometimes a pained retreat by characters from the necessity to create every day who they are and to create every day their world. The problem is not basically one of knowledge in these cases: it is the problem of existence. It has become obvious that reality is not independent of the self in Kleist's works. Also, a seemingly paradoxical relationship between the self and reality exists: the self, through its activity, struggles to control and mold reality, yet the self also seems to attempt to remove itself to an aloof distance from the reality which painfully impinges on it, to free itself in extreme cases from existing in any relationship to reality at all. These paradoxical tugs on the self require further examination.

Chapter 6

THE AUTONOMY OF SELF AND REALITY

Kleist works very little from theory in his works, but instead
primarily from the concreteness of individuals. He fashions
three-dimensional people in unique contexts of social and
interpersonal relationships, people who with few exceptions are
plausible as individuals whether Kleist casts them into bizarre
predicaments or not. Kleist is undeniably fascinated with extreme
situations, and he may capture the reader's attention through an
unheard-of occurrence -- in his dramas as well as in his novellas.
Nevertheless, the reader is not presented with the disruption of a
world that is familiar by virtue of its normality. Rather, the
reader must take some care to consider that he is being confronted
with universes where "normal" situations are never problem-free,
where the mechanics of interaction in the status quo ante are one
of the very things that Kleist is exploring and examining, where
normality is frequently a surface beneath which characters exist
in private worlds that are very different from the surface.

Life itself is a dreadful and difficult business for most of
Kleist's characters, and Kleist experiments with the ways in which
individuals try to exist and to survive -- with and without
external stresses. It is not just that Kleist chooses extreme

situations, as Dorrit Cohn correctly says, out of a "belief that they reveal more about human nature than the norm itself."[1] It is unwise to focus solely on what sets his characters off into a crisis or to focus on the external extremes. Kleist's fascination with the event frequently demonstrates his search for those incidents that provide a glimpse into human reactions to the world and to other people and into the manner in which his characters simply try to exist. "Normality" is a term which must be qualified when used to refer to the interactions between Kleist's characters, because in his works even the mechanics of interaction in everyday matters can be riddled with bizarre problems. In his works Kleist does not give us the confrontation between one heroic consciousness and a solid, antagonistic reality. He gives us realities formed and molded by contingent characters whose engagement with the world and with other people is frequently insecure.

Reality is not in itself the antagonist of Kleist's characters. The first chapters sought to demonstrate that Kleist consistently relativizes reality -- not by destroying the foundations of what is physically real, but by showing the internal mechanics of the self altering its experience of reality. It would be wrong to endow Kleist's reality with the validity and solidity of a vital force in opposition to his characters. The nature of reality shifts with the manipulation of it by the characters who, in the process, gain control over it.

The characters certainly are not confronted with fate -- they create their own lot more than is generally acknowledged.[2] To be sure, there are catastrophes in Kleist's works which lie beyond human control. However, the external catastrophes such as earthquakes and accidental drownings -- which, not incidentally, tend to occur before the story begins or at the fringes of the narrative presentation -- slip from the center of the reader's concern because the human-caused catastrophes, based on the mental acrobatics of the characters, form the actual engines of the stories. An external fate seems not to come into question here at all.[3]

The structuring of events is obviously of some concern, but a differentiated view must be taken. The apparent capriciousness of events should not be taken as a sign that Kleist is making a statement to the effect that the nature of the universe is one of capricious antagonism or of fortuitous circumstance that somehow is aimed at individuals in order to bring about their wretched lots. Kleist continually asserts the ultimate freedom of his characters; on the level of experience itself and on the level of action, the characters create who and what they are.

The origin of these external brutal circumstances lies in Kleist himself, which suits perfectly the experimental nature of his works. It is as if he were saying, as he proceeds inductively with a plot, "how would my characters react if confronted with these adverse circumstances?" And Kleist may follow one fortuitous circumstance with another, forcing his characters to cope with them. For example, the "Findling" is a work especially marked by the presence of coincidence. At every turn, something "happens" to occur which moves the story to a new stage. But this is hardly a chain of coincidences coherently linked together to produce a fatal necessity. One is far more justified in taking Kleist to task for producing a work which is so contrived. He often appears to have written inductively, proceeding from flashes of fancy and from sudden ideas, and he does not actually intend to portray a cosmos where individuals' fates are predetermined. As one example of his inductive progression in the "Findling," Piachi, upon discovering Nicolo in Elvire's chambers, removes a whip from the wall. Now, the attempt to use the whip on Nicolo certainly escalates the confrontation to a violent level, but one would be foolish to conclude that such a coincidental presence of a whip was fated. It is there, it seems reasonable to assume, because Kleist decides he wants it there. Nor should one assume, as does one critic, that the presence of the whip is motivated on a literary level -- as a sign of Piachi's brutal management of the household.[4] In the first place, it is disputable whether Piachi can be made out to be the arch villain of this work where all characters share responsibility for the morally debilitating atmosphere of the house. On the more practical plane, a bedroom is an odd location for a whip, even in Kleist's worlds. Elvire certainly does not seem to use it on herself, and since Piachi does not share bedchambers with her it seems unlikely that he would store it in hers. The whip is simply an unmotivated presence and hardly belongs to a systematic pattern of Zufall, much less of fate.

Kleist inductively writes himself into such corners more than once in his works. In the "Verlobung," another unexpected but convenient bedroom accoutrement appears in the form of ropes, with which Toni can bind Gustav as Congo Hoango unexpectedly returns. In Käthchen, Theobald's blacksmith shop is located on the second floor, a fact we discover when Käthchen hurtles out the window in blind pursuit of Strahl. Presumably, a reasonable motivation for the location of the blacksmith shop takes second place to the desire to demonstrate the lack of self-regard where her overriding love is concerned.

The reader must take some care when viewing the various disruptions in the lives of Kleist's characters. There are, clearly, occurrences whose origins lie outside any claim to human causality. These events of circumstance are either a secondary concern to Kleist, events which set the story in motion and subsequently recede from the center of the reader's attention, or, as in the examples above, the causality may originate in Kleist himself, who at times moves his experiments along with goading coincidence. Kleist focuses on the psychological and existential plane in the stressful situations in which his characters are put.

The subjectively truer, if at times less real, threats to characters come often not from the externally verifiable catastrophes which confront the characters but rather from other individuals who form the environment and pose a threat to other people in Kleist's works.

The causality which the characters believe in most is a human causality. Ultimately, it is people of whom the characters are most aware, not events. The notorious lack of ability to relate to other individuals, a quality shared by most of Kleist's characters, does not mean that they are unaware of others. Other people, in fact, are precisely what continually thwart the sovereignty of the self by refusing to validate how the self has ordered its experience. Many of Kleist's central characters become almost pathologically aware of the fact that what they are and what is "real" is dependent on other people.

This phenomenological aspect is apparent in virtually every work of Kleist. Characters are excruciatingly aware of their appearance and their image, that is, how others will understand their appearance. In Schroffenstein, for example, appearance and the visual element is the core of everyone's experience. Even Sylvius, who is blind, prefers to use visual clues to understand or apprehend the inner content of others, rather than to use the other senses at his disposal. He wants to know what Agnes feels at one point and asks, "sprich, ist sie rot?"(436) Throughout the play, the characters are conscious of an audience to their exterior selves, an audience that may not even be definable, as when Sylvester states generally, "Wir, wir Menschen fallen ja nicht für Geld, auch nicht zur Schau. --Doch sollen wir stets des Anschauns würdig aufstehen"(967-9). The appearances one supplies to the outside are not merely important; they are literally essential, since the judgment of the person is based on others' perceptions of the individual, not on any static content of a person's soul. The outer self determines existence in many cases, regardless of what an individual holds to be his or her true nature. Guiskard's refusal to utter the possibility of his being ill is not only an evasive maneuver for himself, an unwillingness to admit his own illness; it is an attempt to control the equally important assessment by others. He displays controlled fury when he learns of Abälard's indiscretion with the crowd; and the preceding verbal duel between Robert and Abälard had been a battle to sway and control the crowd. The enormous tension in the last scenes of the fragment is between what Guiskard attempts to make the crowd believe and the familiy's apprehension that the facade they present will not be accepted. Reality takes second place to mere perception, because reality is what others say is real.

In moral as well as in existential contexts, what the characters hold to be their true nature is vulnerable to and dependent on others to a great degree, and this theme lies near the center of many works. The discrepancy between inner knowledge of oneself and others' "knowledge" of who and what one is, is the center of Sylvester's plight in confrontation with Aldöbern, of the Graf's and Julietta's problems, of Littegarde's and Rotbart's legal and moral confrontation, of Amphitryon's and of Homburg's identity crises.

This causality of knowledge emanates from a human source of ordering; it originates with the givers of meaning. Neither a divine causality nor the causality of natural law seems to supply order in Kleist's works. Events -- catastrophes or otherwise -- hover unattached until someone fixes the event; and further, the events are invariably attached to people. The event-catastrophe in Kleist's works that is so frequently cited as the obvious model for an external catastrophe breaking over the heads of the characters -- namely, the earthquake in Chili -- reveals itself to

be, in experiential terms, a model of human causality. The earthquake can not be grasped by the citizens at first, and it gains
meaning -- and a cause -- not when it is attributed to God, for
that intermediate stage is passed through very quickly, but when
it is attributed to the sin of Jeronimo and Josephe. The paradigm
used to explain the earthquake is not one of God's will but rather
one that orders in terms of ultimate human causality.[5] God, in
effect, ceases to be the unmoved mover. Josephe attributes the
event entirely to divine causality, of course, but her positive
interpretation of the earthquake as God's grace proves to be
false, or at least false in practical terms, for her
interpretation finds no credence with others. Whatever the
earthquake is, for the characters it is what they say it is in
human terms, and that is what makes the story move.

Similarly, nature itself is not a controlling force nor even
a neutral backdrop of existence for Kleist's characters. Man as
the controlling force over nature is evoked in imagery which shows
nature to be subordinate to the ordering power of man. As a
symbolic representation of this, when Agnes first appears on the
stage in Schroffenstein, for example, she is engaged in arranging
and ordering the natural randomness of flowers into a wreath for a
specifically human reason -- to create an aesthetic object of
human perception:

> Stundenlang hab ich
> Gesonnen, wie ein jedes einzeln Blümchen
> Zu stellen, wie das unscheinbarste selbst
> Zu nutzen sei, damit Gestalt und Farbe
> Des Ganzen seine Wirkung tue ... Da, nimm
> Ihn hin. Sprich: er gefällt mir; so ist er
> Bezahlt. (719-26)

Likewise, when Sylvester had first entered the stage in the preceding scene which was touched on above, he had spoken of the ordering of his garden:

> Ausreißen ist ein froh Geschäft,
> Geschiehts um etwas Besseres zu pflanzen.
> Denk dir das junge Volk von Bäumen, die,
> Wenn wir vorbeigehn, wie die Kinder tanzen,
> Und uns mit ihren Blütenaugen ansehn
> Es wird dich freuen, Hans, du kannsts mir glauben. (490-5)

Man is used to explain nature in metaphorical terms, not natural phenomena to clarify human action. The metaphorical pattern in these passages and in others draws attention to itself because man is the metaphor's referent, not nature: the underlying order of things is not the order of natural law but of human presence as the origin of order. In Penthesilea, to choose a striking example of metaphorical usage, especially when compared to that of Homer's Iliad, which is clearly otherwise the stylistic model for Kleist, the natural metaphors are inextricably interlaced with the individuals they are attached to. Homer's style is almost totally free of metaphors; his placement of man in the order of nature functions entirely on the level of similes -- for Homer, Achilles may race across a field like a thundering storm which moves across a plain. In Kleist's Penthesilea, Achilles and Penthesilea are thundering storms that collide. The two characters are the cosmic forces that cause external order to wane to insignificance.

Nature does not enjoy an independent existence for Kleist's characters, and it cannot itself supply guiding causal events as far as the characters are concerned. The natural order and universal ordering concepts are repeatedly shown to be non-

functional, or at the most, of secondary importance for the
characters. At times, external order, natural or otherwise, is
violently debunked as an artificial construct because it is an
individual's internal order. In <u>Schroffenstein</u>, Rupert says in
the first scene of the play:

> Doch nichts mehr von Natur.
> Ein hold ergötzend Märchen ists der Kindheit,
> Der Menschheit von den Dichtern, ihren Ammen,
> Erzählt.

and he continues:

>   Vertrauen, Unschuld, Treue, Liebe,
> Religion, der Götter Furcht, sind wie
> Die Tiere, welche reden. (42-7)

This really has nothing to do with the inscrutability of natural
or divine law, but rather with the absence of it -- for man, and
as an experienced causal force. The environment is not an orderly
backdrop of existence, rooted in the absolute, immutable, real,
and credible substance of reality; it is not an external reliable
structure of form and law underpinning the entire plane of man's
experience; it is not divine order. It is not only reality that
is relative, but causality and the most basic moral values as
well.

Nevertheless, neither for Rupert nor for other Kleistian
characters is the environment a chaotic process of negation of
order, nor is it random disorder. The causal forces are located
and determined by the transmitted orderings of others, by that
seemingly magic power of the mind to determine what is. Nature
and external order cannot manifest themselves as a neutral context
of human experience. Man as the prime mover of events, circum-

stances, and appearances is at the center of the stage. Man, in fact, is the stage. With no guarantor of meaning in God or in nature, Kleist allows the self to take over.

The battle for the control of reality is transferred to the level of consciousness in Kleist's works; that is where meaning is formed. It is there that everything of substance occurs in these worlds, for even if what occurs there is less real, it is more true. It is this combination of concerns which makes an approach to the discussion of the nature of Kleist's characters inseparable from a discussion of metaphysics: in these worlds, where words mold and replace reality, language is the order of the universe; knowledge is an act with all the force of an act of the will or with all the force of a physical act; what is known is that which is; and in these worlds, where one is what others say one is, language creates identity.[6] The battle to control reality is of necessity not confined to the individual's ordering of his or her own experience, for the motivating impulse here is not the question of can we know, but rather of who will control what is known, what is real.

None of Kleist's characters is solipsistic. Rather, they seem to be possessed by a painful and even pathological sensitivity to the power which resides in the very subjectivity of others. The battle goes beyond the compulsive need to control one's own experience; the battle extends further, from the need to control the content and the knowledge of others to the need to control the experience of others as well. It is apparent in

Kleist's works that the interaction between two individuals is not only a social encounter but frequently also an existential confrontation. The deluding of the self which characterized the manipulations of language and experience in the examples cited in the preceding chapters has its necessary complement in the deluding of others through the manipulation of _their_ experience. Others are the entire significant environment of Kleist's individuals. The jockeying for control of what is, is at times on such a basic level as to be equated with a battle for existence of the self, certainly a battle for sanity. For Kleist, the distinction between sanity and existence is often a useless one to make, because many of his characters are fragile enough to have not only their sanity shaken when their experience and ordering of the world is called into question; their whole sense of who they are is threatened at the same time. As noted in the example of Sylvester's confrontation with Aldöbern, Kleist's characters seem to feel that they are entirely too vulnerable in their own experience and identity. The victories that his characters seek are not moral victories but rather the successful defense of fragile experience or the successful manipulation of the experience of others. The problems which confront Kleist's characters are never solely the result of internal conflicts.[7] This is the battle by characters to control their own experience by controlling the experience of others.

Chapter 7

THE MANIPULATION OF THE OTHER: ROLES AND ROLE MODELS

It is perhaps most obvious in Kleist's most threatened characters,
such as Penthesilea or Amphitryon, that these characters resist
the separation of self and world, that they feel that the world is
still an extension of the self, but this is apparent in the
thinking of even lighter characters as well, such as Sosias or as
Adam in Der Zerbrochene Krug. What characterizes this resistance
is the magical naming of reality, the making objects conform to
thought rather than the reverse.   The feeling that these
characters desperately want the world to be theirs, that the world
is a part of them, is manifest in their very use of language in
the word games that are inextricably connected with the self's
existence.   When a character such as Penthesilea utters a wish in
rage or joy, as, for example, in the ninth scene -- "Daß der ganze
Frühling verdorrte! Daß der Stern, auf dem wir atmen, geknickt,
gleich dieser Rosen einer, läge!"(1226-8) -- it is not a mere
projection of feeling.   It is an incantation, a seizing of the
world in the grips of the mind, a reduction of a separate world of
objects to parts of her self.   The natural world does not gain
independence from her desires.   A similar but oppositely directed
command uses the same imagery of nature as an extension of her:

in an earlier scene she had bidden, "Hebt euch, ihr Frühlings-
blumen, seinem <Achilles> Fall, daß seiner Glieder keines sich
verletze"(861-2). What must be noted in this -- and as a system
of language it is clearly an extraordinary, and an extraordinarily
unhealthy, use of language -- is that real objects do not lose
reality; the problem is a psychological one: objects are absorbed
into the power of the self; or rather, the self tries to absorb
objects back into itself.[1] Further -- and this is particularly a
problem for Penthesilea, though it exists for nearly every one of
Kleist's characters who feels threatened -- the world of objects
includes other people. The subjectivity of others represents not
merely a barrier but a threat. This is the cause of the
reification of others; this is why the subjectivity of others is
reduced to an object. It is frequently difficult to ascertain
where an incapacity to see the "you-ness" of another leaves off
and an unwillingness or even a fear of doing so begins.

In _Penthesilea_ this really is identical to Sartre's battle of
the sexes. Penthesilea kills the other: she destroys Achilles
physically, and she actually eats him in destroying him,
symbolically absorbing him.[2] She also mentally "destroys"
Prothoe, the only other person to threaten her with love, and the
objective correlative of Achilles' murder is the moment when
Penthesilea draws her bow and aims at Prothoe until distracted by
someone else. Penthesilea's mind in that scene does not see
Prothoe as Prothoe but as a dead thing, an object.

Important in this is that while the subjectivity of other
individuals may be denied or destroyed, it _is_ noted, which is

precisely what provokes such a violent response in Penthesilea, probably the most vulnerable of Kleist's characters. But even in the cases of characters who do not feel as directly threatened at the core of their selves, the reduction of the other people's subjectivity to an object is apparent. There is a near paradox inherent in this reduction, for on the one hand characters are, as stated, very aware of the subjectivity of others and that they themselves exist as an object in the light of the other's consciousness; on the other hand, others are seen as objects. The point of unity in this apparent paradox lies in the subjectivity of others: the self can control the subjectivity of the other by controlling the objects of the other's consciousness; others can be manipulated by modifying and controlling what they know, by modifying and controlling their environment.

If individuals are capable of self-delusion, they are also capable of deluding others. As this chapter will attempt to demonstrate, Kleist's characters continually attempt to control the meaning of events for others, to control the rules by which reality is formed by others, and to control how others view themselves.

One of the hallmarks of Kleist's characters is the shabby way in which they treat each other, even, or perhaps especially, the ones they love most. Gundolf, without analysis, appropriately called this "das halb gequälte halb lüsterne Lauern, die Lust am Katz- und Mausspielen."[3] Toying with others, disdainfully and insensitively subjecting them to various forms of emotional and

physical abuse is so pervasive in Kleist's works as to remove all
possibility of coincidence. It seems to mar even otherwise
sympathetic characters, which has been cause for some puzzlement
for critics. When at the end of Käthchen, for example, Strahl
cruelly leads both Kunigunde and Käthchen to believe that he
actually intends to marry Kunigunde, his lack of regard for
Käthchen surprises us even if his trick on Kunigunde does not. In
trying to come to terms with this as an isolated instance, one
might well be forced to explain the lover's behavior on an
inappropriate level. Fricke in this instance decides that
Strahl's behavior is a retarding moment, Kleist's creation of an
aesthetic distance for the reader who, now sure of the real
outcome, can enjoy the greatness of the hero's victory in peace.[4]
Such an interpretation, however, fails to take note of how this
sporting with others is a trait that is shared by several of
Kleist's characters, some of whom actually enjoy it, others of
whom feel compelled to do it out of some dire necessity.
Kunigunde and Hermann seem to relish their control of others, and
the Elector in Homburg plays his unnecessary jokes on Homburg in
the last as well as in the first scene. The Graf, Toni, and
Gustav, on the other hand, are motivated to control others by the
pressure of circumstances.

The manipulation of others occurs in various ways which
obviously overlap. Characters attempt to control others and
reality by saying, in essence, "you are who I say you are,"
"things are the way I say they are," and "I am who I say I am."
In this section the first two of these will be examined.

This system of speaking, of controlling what is, is a bizarre system of interaction which does -- and yet does not -- respect the subjectivity of others. The manipulating character recognizes the power that lies in the subjectivity of others but at the same time seeks to control that subjectivity as if it were a thing. The manipulating character attempts to control what is, by controlling knowledge, for what is "known" in these worlds can supplant what really is there. This entire aspect was developed in the preceding chapters in a limited fashion, but in those examples the quality of deluding oneself through the manipulation of experience was emphasized. The deluding of others and the manipulation of their experience is equally pervasive.

At times these two aspects of the manipulation of experience are inseparable. In the verbal duel between Sylvester and Aldöbern in Schroffenstein, for example, Sylvester's attempts to mold the flow and the content of the encounter clearly emanate from the necessity to keep his own knowledge of self and reality intact in order to prevent his being named, and transformed into, a murderer. But the battle is joined over which of the two verbal realities will win out: Sylvester must try to force Aldöbern to change his accusation. In order to mold reality Sylvester must try to mold a person first. The entire dynamic of the scene is based on that manipulative process, in fact, because Sylvester's reaction is triggered by his horror at the realization that Aldöbern has altered him -- named him as one would name a thing -- and altered his whole world as well. This is a plea for collusion, as in many other cases. Rupert's harangue in Schroffenstein and Congo Hoango's tirades against the whites in the "Verlobung" reflect not only the reduction of phenomena by the speakers, but also the reduction of people by denying their humanity. Their speech not only reflects the fact that they have reorganized the nature of other people in their environment: i.e., that they are persuading themselves that their adversaries are less than human; it also reflects Rupert's and Hoango's attempt to sway the will of their audience as well. Rupert may himself be lost in his wild vision, but he clearly also intends to enthuse his listeners and direct the course of their thought and action, and Rupert, like others who manipulate those around them, uses the devices of rhetoric and oratory at his disposal to guide the thought of others. His vision becomes concrete, and this aspect of his rhetoric is obviously propaganda such as one could find during virtually any war. He manipulates his people into the "knowledge" that the people at Warwand are their enemies, that they are less than human, that they deserve to be destroyed, that it would be no moral crime to destroy them. Rupert manipulates his own experience of what is, and he manipulates what his people "know" as well.

Kleist is quite aware of this political dimension of mind control. In the "Verlobung" he reveals the reduction of others and the removal of others' humanness to be a fundamental cause, and result, of racism and prejudice. Congo Hoango is, within the limits of the story, the creator of the dog metaphor for whites and Creoles. This name is used by Congo himself, of course, and whenever anyone else uses it, Congo is mentioned as the source of that knowledge, as the source of validity for that reduction. Congo, it must also be noted, is himself the victim of racism; his leadership in the rebellion is the assertion of his own autonomy after a lifetime of being oppressed and treated as less than an autonomous moral being. The self is viewed by these characters as the causal element in relation to the bits of reality around the character and in relation to others. They know the power they possess over others.

It is the others who are stuff, the objects to be manipulated. It is the others who are so often forced to collude, willy-nilly, in the formation and acceptance of a posited reality. The private orderings of reality are in fact strengthened when confirmed by others. Gustav's placement of the role of Mariane on Toni in the "Verlobung" is a manipulation of Toni that serves to create a pocket of safety for him in his own mind. When she accepts that role, or seems to, his illusion becomes substantial for him. Likewise, in Schroffenstein, Jeronimus, a figure who belongs to neither Warwand nor Rossitz, is a remarkable catalyst for the continuance of the delusions of various characters. He seems to have no personality at all. His amorphous character is influenced and determined by those characters in his immediate surroundings, because he believes everything anyone tells him.[5] Swayed to the party of Warwand when he is at Warwand and to that of Rossitz when he is at Rossitz, he falls alternatively under the sway of competing arrangements of reality. Seemingly lacking any internal essence himself, he cannot see below the surface of those with whom he must deal. His influence on the events of the story

-- events that occur as shifting orderings of reality -- is considerable. Because he readily accepts arguments from others and vacillates so readily, his acceptance of another's arguments incidentally serves to strengthen the other person's conviction of being correct. He declares his alliance to Rossitz at the beginning and helps to solidify Ottokar's resolve to destroy Warwand, and his elaborate creation of an insidious plot by Rossitz against Warwand later serves to arouse more mistrust in Warwand and even brings doubts to Sylvester's mind for the first time(1183ff.).

Jeronimus' malleability -- really, the malleability of his experience, of what he knows to be true -- is the plight of a subjectivity that is too weak to confront another subjectivity successfully. Even masses of people fall under the sway of the manipulation of what is. It is the ugliness of the manipulated mob at Rossitz that recurs in other guises in other works -- in the "Verlobung" it is the revolutionary mob in France which acts out of one vision, destroying all who do not conform and confess to that vision; it is also the two sides of the revolution in Santo Domingo, each locked into an induced reductive vision; it is the mob in "Erdbeben" which is incited to a murderous frenzy by the canon who, "im Flusse priesterlicher Beredsamkeit"(155), demonstrates that it was sin, with Jeronimo and Josephe as the prime example, which was the cause behind the cosmic forces unleashed on Santiago. The rhythm of vocabulary in the canon's exposition of the causal mechanics of the earthquake is Kleist's underscoring of his "explanation" as verbal construct. "Er schilderte ...," the harangue begins, and the threefold recurrence of the verb "nannte" is a fixing of the role of Jeronimo and Josephe(155-6). The canon's speech climaxes in a curse, parallel to the curse in the first scene of Schroffenstein, which fixed Warwand as the archenemy which had to be destroyed.

In Die Hermannsschlacht virtually everyone is prey to the machinations of Hermann, who manipulates people, appearances, and events in a skillful orchestration of everything that affects his vision of what Germany ought to be. Hermann stands sovereign at the center of all action in the play, pulling strings in a tightly controlled drama of historical movement. He forces Thusnelda to play a false role with Ventidius and thus manipulates them both. But even more significantly, in act III, scene 2, Hermann sets a false game in motion that moves Germans and Romans like chess pieces, a game that fundamentally alters the image -- and thus, obviously, the reality -- of the Romans in the Germans' eyes. Three captains report isolated encounters between Germans and units of the Roman army, or individual excesses of Roman soldiers. Hermann takes the basic information supplied by the captains and alters the meaning of the events and sends out the fabrications for general consumption by the Germans. The first report -- that three of Hermann's settlements had been plundered -- is changed by Hermann through simple exaggeration. "Heimlich und freudig," Hermann commands the "rumor" be spread that it had been seven settlements(900). The fact that this is misrepresentation, that Hermann's story is a creation which does not correspond to reality, does not trouble him at all, of course, any more than it is an issue when he fabricates a murder out of the second captain's report and has the story spread that an angry father was buried alive by the Romans after his wife and child had been killed. From the third captain's report of the Romans' suppression of a rebellion after the Romans had unintentionally cut down an ancient and sacred oak tree, Hermann creates the story that the prisoners had been forced to kneel in the dirt before Zeus, whom Hermann calls the Romans' "God of Atrocities"(932-4). The progression is a crescendo, moving from the destruction of physical property to the destruction of lives and freedom to an assault on the Germanic gods themselves. The threat of the Romans, though by no means harmless, is painted as a threat to absolutely everything of value -- to property, to family, to life, to the human spirit, to the very gods, all this at a time when negotiations with the Romans are supposedly in progress. It is a wide-reaching game of "Hermann sagt-"(901).

There is a clear callousness in Hermann, who manipulates his own compatriots as well as the Romans. First, with the aid of Eginhardt, he induces the messengers to collude in his strategy; the captains are led away by the arm in a visual analogue to their being led to Hermann's "truth." His "knowledge" becomes their knowledge: "Ich hab es von dir selbst gehört!" says Hermann to the third captain, suggesting how the captain should play along, how the captain should vouch for the validity of the fabrication when he repeats the story.

The last measure taken by Hermann in the scene is the crowning touch to his plan. He arranges to have a band of his own men disguise themselves as Romans, follow behind the Roman army, and burn, plunder and lay waste to the countryside. After creating Greuelmärchen, stories which he anticipates will be accepted as reality, he sets out to validate the stories himself -- and at the expense of his own people.

In the patterns Kleist establishes, the manipulation of phenomenal bits is seldom separate from the manipulation of people. Events and words, as has repeatedly been shown, are constant prey to the ordering power of individuals, but people fare no better. They are moved about, their experience and their very selves are manipulated, reduced to phenomenal bits also. This is apparent even on the physical level, and it functions as a natural symbol to have characters pushed, pulled, and tugged, as they are in the "Verlobung" or in Hermannschlacht -- or actually bound, as Gustav is by Toni when he is unconscious. And even though Hermann may fabricate a story about the death of a man, it is more fascinating, in a horrifying sort of way, to observe Piachi in the "Findling." After Piachi has forbidden Nicolo to communicate with Xaviera Tartini, Piachi intercepts a letter from Nicolo to her, and Piachi's next actions, by their excess, determine the destructive direction the story soon takes. After tearing the note from the maid's hands, "halb mit List, halb mit Gewalt," he sets a bizarre plan in motion in order to punish and humiliate Nicolo(205). First, in letter form, he assumes the guise of Xaviera and schedules a rendezvous with Nicolo. Then, in a cruel twist, instead of allowing Xaviera to appear at the assignation or appearing himself, Piachi delivers the corpse of

Nicolo's deceased wife, Constanze, to the appointment. This is at
best a tasteless excess on the part of Piachi; he maneuvers
appearances, people, and the corpse of Constanze as if they were
stage props. It is not only on the literal level that he moves
dead bodies about; similarly, Piachi takes equally little note of
Nicolo as a living, feeling being. Nicolo is of course outraged
at the public degradation he suffers, and the incident sets in
motion Nicolo's own deceit and nefarious subterfuge.

The manipulation of another's subjectivity and person is akin
to killing them. That the other is a subject with its own world
is not taken seriously even if it is noted; the other person
becomes an extension of the controlling individual. In the case
of Nicolo, we note the speed with which he is shown his "place"
and who he ought to be upon arriving in Rome as a child. He is put
in the position of having to replace, even be, Paolo:

> In Rom stellte ihn Piachi ... Elviren ... vor, welche
> sich zwar nicht enthalten konnte, bei dem Gedanken an
> Paolo, ihren kleinen Stiefsohn, den sie sehr geliebt
> hatte, herzlich zu weinen; gleichwohl aber den Nicolo,
> so fremd und steif er auch vor ihr stand, an ihre Brust
> drückte, ihm das Bette, worin jener geschlafen hatte,
> zum Lager anwies, und sämtliche Kleider desselben zum
> Geschenk machte. (201)

Nicolo is literally put in the position of filling a role,
complete with props and costumes, and of meeting quite definite
expectations from the beginning.[6] In the description of his
formative years we hear nothing of what he did, only of what his
step-parents did to, for, and with him, and of what happened to
him. It is, the reader discovers, only in his private life,
hidden from his step-parents, that he asserts himself as an

individual. Elsewhere, in the presence of Piachi and Elvire, he is forced to play his expected role, in effect to cease to be himself.[7]

Likewise, in the "Verlobung" it is Gustav's grasping of Toni's hands, his enclosing her body in his arms, and the like, which are the images that one recalls most easily when one thinks of his actions with her. Like his naming her "mein liebes Mädchen," these are, to be sure, attempts to order the environment, to create a sense of security for himself, but they are also a visual reflection of his manipulation of Toni. The grasping, handling possessiveness of Gustav is at least in part a conscious attempt to probe the mind and intentions of Toni and discover, perhaps uncover, her real nature. His need for safety and comfort is inseparable from his attempt to seduce her. He suspects that Toni is only artifice, and while he is genuinely attracted to her, his method of proceeding in this initial encounter with her is also calculated and emanates from his own self and from his own designs. His seduction of her occurs through gestures and words. The somewhat biased narrator tells us:

> Er ergriff sie ... bei der Hand, und da er gar richtig
> schloß, daß es nur ein Mittel gab, zu erprüfen, ob das
> Mädchen ein Herz habe oder nicht, so zog er sie auf
> seinen Schoß nieder und fragte sie: "ob sie schon einem
> Bräutigam verlobt wäre?" (172)

He embraces her, strokes her hair, rocks her on his knees, kisses her. And his words during all this are suggestive; he tells her that in his country, a girl of fourteen years seven weeks is old enough to marry; he asks her how old she is, and she answers that she is fifteen -- significantly, a fact which he had already ascertained earlier from Babekan; he asks the more pointed suggestive question, "ihr scherzend ins Ohr geflüstert: ob es vielleicht ein Weißer sein müsse, der ihre Gunst davon tragen solle?"(173) This somewhat tasteless display of handling and suggestion, of physical and verbal manipulation, shows a definite confidence, a sense of control, an ego that operates on premises of male dominance and white superiority. Having satisfied himself that she is not a cold and heinous traitor, he kisses her as a sign of reconciliation and, inexplicably, forgiveness: "<Er> drückte ... gleichsam zum Zeichen der Aussöhnung und Vergebung, einen Kuß auf ihre Stirn"(173). His notion that she is a treacherous woman was, from the point of view of what he actually knows, a creation in his own mind, so it is inexplicable that he should "forgive" her; he is forgiving her for <u>his</u> suspicions, a phantom of his own creation.

This scene is loaded with complex irony. The suspicions which are manufactured in Gustav's mind do in fact initially coincide with the truth, for Toni has indeed set out to trap him in this encounter. There is also irony in his decision that Toni is safe; he is again correct, but for the wrong reasons and at the wrong time -- she has hardly always been innocent, and she is at the moment not yet so; it is only after he recounts the story of Mariane that she is completely moved to renounce her past. His forgiveness of her, then, is ironically also appropriate even though it is based on false assumptions on his part. Finally, his belief that he is seducing Toni turns out to be accurate though his ultimate feeling that the "seduction" was, under the circumstances, unnecessary is definitely misplaced. Gustav is connecting with Toni and with the truth but on a level and in a sequence that does not at all represent a genuine encounter, and the reader can easily appreciate the tragic irony of the scene, an irony which lies in Gustav's belief that he is in control of events. This is the one thing which proves to be least true of his precarious situation in the novella. The whole sequence is an example of self-delusion as well as of delusion of Toni, and he succeeds in seducing himself as well as her.

Here, as in so many of Kleist's works, sex and the battle between the sexes represent the manipulation by one person to gain control over another. There is not necessarily a "we" involved in the love relationships or sexual relationships in Kleist's texts. The relationship between Penthesilea and Achilles is almost paradigmatic for this problem, but it occurs elsewhere in other forms. Kunigunde employs her false charms to manipulate all the men she has use for; Amphitryon sees his wife virtually as an extension of himself, as one of his prizes; the Graf in the "Marquise von O..." rapes Julietta -- while she is unconscious; it is difficult to ascertain whether Nicolo is being more sensitive or less sensitive than the Graf when, after carrying the unconscious Elvire to the bed in the corner of her bedroom, he attempts to revive her "mit heißen Küssen" to her breast and lips before the anticipated rape(213); Ventidius pays court to Thusnelda in Hermannschlacht not least because he wants some of her blond hair as a prize to take back to Rome, and Hermann uses her as one of his tools in the war against the Romans. Characters who love freely, openly, and for the other person are unusual in Kleist's works; Prothoe in _Penthesilea_ and Natalie in _Homburg_ are hardly the norm.

The "thingness" of the other is clearly not something inherent in being the other: it is a quality that is manufactured in the consciousness of the manipulating self. People are not so impenetrable by nature. The lack of ability and desire to relate and to open oneself is ultimately a failure not of language or of perception but of the self as subject: the other is simply not regarded on a deep level as being human or as being a subject with a world of experience that has any serious claim to validity. This is not to say, of course, that characters make it easy for others to know them. An equally complicating trait of many of Kleist's characters is the manner in which they erect barriers and facades in front of themselves, frequently making it impossible for anyone else to know them or their inner world. This aspect of skewed interaction will be discussed in detail later.

First, however, the gamesmanship involving the assigning of meaning to people and phenomena can be discussed in a somewhat broader context. However much the characters described above attempt to treat the world as an extension of the self, Kleist always brings them up hard against the worlds of other people. It is not so much an immovable real world that is at issue here, for Kleist gives ample evidence that in his works a solid world of _things_ is of far less consequence than an unorganized world of phenomena that are relativized and ordered by the causal and

manipulative self. Kleist clearly does not view reality as a
world of things but rather as a system of rules, as relative
structures.

Kleist's individuals are constantly forced to realize that
they exist in someone else's space, and it is an uncomfortable,
often bitter awakening for them. This is represented by
characters' being moved physically into a new space, such as
Nicolo's finding himself in the place of Paolo, or Gustav's
finding himself in the place of the murdered Villeneuve, or
Amphitryon's finding himself displaced as Alkmene's husband and as
king of Thebes. Characters also have their position in the world
shifted through a change in the linguistic space they occupy, such
as Sylvester's being renamed a murderer by Aldöbern and a villain
by Jeronimus, or, in the "Zweikampf," Littegarde's being accused
of leading a second and immoral life. Many characters suddenly
become aware that they no longer occupy the position in the world
they had thought they occupied. They are abruptly made aware that
the structure of things has changed, and that someone else is
controlling or manipulating the flow of events and reality. It is
awareness of this "someone else" and the fight to control the
structure of things that are of interest here.

This fight underlies many of the interactions discussed thus
far, but of moment here is the element of deceit dominating this
aspect of gamesmanship, the way in which Kleist's characters move
their rhetorical arsenals and their physical actions to best
effect in battles which take place in and for the hearts and minds
of other characters. It is not a fight that takes place in an

environment where the self can develop and express itself. Individuals do not meet and interact in any genuine way; instead, forms of behavior and facades meet, assess the other, and join battle. There is an astonishing element of surface involved in the way characters engage each other in these earnest games and in the way they attempt to control the "rules" of the games.

Frequently there is a roundabout way in which characters interact. In Schroffenstein, when Jeronimus, now more on the side of Warwand, returns to Rossitz in act III to try to convince Rupert to have a meeting with Sylvester, Rupert has him killed. Now, Rupert could simply have him executed, of course, but Rupert goes about it in a far more complicated manner. The immediate cause of Rupert's outrage, of course, is that the herald Aldöbern was slain by Sylvester's people in violation of the herald's right of safe passage. For Rupert the message of that act is unmistakable: war has been declared; the request for a meeting is a treacherous sham; Jeronimus is the agent of Sylvester, attempting to maneuver him into a trap. Jeronimus _is_ indeed less than honest in this scene, feigning suspicion of Sylvester and playing the role of a neutral observer, which he is not, entirely.

Theoretically in a weaker position when confronted with a manipulating Jeronimus, Rupert walks on the stage and seizes control of the course of dialogue. He does not confront Jeronimus directly, but rather thinks that he is "outplaying" Jeronimus according to the rules of the deceitful game he thinks Warwand is playing. Virtually his first words to Jeronimus are:

> --Vielleicht hast du
> Aufträg an mich, kommst im Geschäft des Friedens,

        Stellst selbst vielleicht die heilige Person
        Des Herolds vor-- ? (1708-11)

Rupert forces a fatal role on Jeronimus. Rupert is, to be sure, ordering events for himself, making some sort of sense out of his environment, but he is not using language to define and fix the essence of his adversary here. He is forcing on Jeronimus a role, a part that Jeronimus is about to play in a drama which Rupert directs. Rupert controls the system of reality and the players in this drama. Jeronimus is clearly placed into a role in which he does not belong, and he clearly has no possibility of defending himself against this definition of himself other than repeating the weak counterstatement, "Als dein Gast komm ich"(1712, also 1781 and 1783). It must be noted that Jeronimus is in no way in the same position as Sylvester had been when he was named a murderer by Aldöbern. Jeronimus' world does not crumble here nor does madness threaten; he is quite aware that he is being threatened physically and that he is being manipulated by Rupert. He simply cannot do anything about it. Rupert establishes a closed system -- based on a model of murder that is taken from the incident at Warwand -- and uses this perverse paradigm of behavior to kill Jeronimus. Though this is a brutal toying with Jeronimus, it is somewhat mitigating when one considers that Rupert actually does have a similar model of treachery in front of him, and he believes that he is rewarding like with like. He is, in a sense, following the rules. It is not insignificant that Rupert chooses as his model what he believes to be his enemy's behavior. Rupert, in this ordering pattern, manages to avoid accepting moral responsibility for the crime he is about to commit; he can say to himself, in effect, that that is the way the game is played.

In a way, Rupert is in an unusually privileged position in this scene. He is in firm physical control of the situation in addition to being in firm linguistic control of the dialogue. He has, in real terms, nothing to fear from Jeronimus, who has no authority and no power at Rossitz save what would be granted to him by Rupert; and of course the latter grants none. This is not unlike Hermann's sway over all that occurs within his sphere of influence. Relatively few of Kleist's characters have such invulnerable sovereignty for more than a few passing moments, however. Most of his characters act from a vulnerable position; they seek to control the behavior of others, the knowledge of others, and the rules by which things occur, because they _must_ try to do so.

When Adam in the _Krug_ plays with the order of things, for example, it is not out of a spirit of sure-footed confidence in either his official position or his glibness. He is trying to save himself. Adam obviously manipulates Eve directly through threats, but he is far more sophisticated, even if transparent and unsuccessful, in the way he manipulates what is known and what will be considered real and be considered true. This manipulation moves into the realm of controlling the rules themselves. He is the comic counterpart to Hermann in many ways. Perhaps the most memorable line Adam brings forth is his response to the challenge presented by the discovery of the unusual footprints leading away from the scene of the crime. The club-foot trail threatens to tear away his guise as innocent moral arbiter and to reveal him to be the quarry everyone is seeking. He suggests:

> Mein Seel, ihr Herrn, die Sache scheint mir ernsthaft ...
> Der Fall, der vorliegt, scheint besonderer
> Erörtrung wert. Ich trage darauf an,
> Bevor wir ein Konklusum fassen,
> Im Haag bei der Synode anzufragen
> Ob das Gericht befugt sei, anzunehmen,
> Daß Beelzebub den Krug zerbrochen hat.   (1742-52)

Having had fairly little success in controlling the flow of events so far, Adam bursts the seams of reality, in essence expanding the realm of the search to the infinite. Of course his request is unsuccessful, but it is a marvelously extravagant attempt to suggest an entirely different system of reality with entirely different causal possibilities. What is a comic episode here, however, is far less comic in other works. If one disregards Adam's bad luck at having Walter present, who undermines his authority, one can see that Adam is, in one respect, the very model of what many of Kleist's characters wish they were. He is, as the chief judicial officer of the village, the sole arbiter of what is admissible as knowledge in this most important trial, of what will be accepted as real and true, of who people are and what events mean.

It is this aspect which links Adam to such characters as Jupiter, Hermann, and Guiskard, and to the would-be manipulators such as the Graf, Gustav, Kunigunde, and even Strahl and Achilles. The desire to control the system and the bits of the system, whatever the emotional or concrete reason peculiar to the character, is so pervasive in the interactions of characters that few of Kleist's works remain untouched by it. There is not a question of malice or evil involved here in most cases, of course, but there is so frequent a dearth of authenticity in characters' behavior and of honesty with others that the concrete mechanism of manipulation exists with and without malicious intent.

In attempting to work their way on the environment, which consists of other minds, characters are so deceitful in the manner in which they represent themselves that it is nearly pointless to distinguish between the manipulation of one's guise and the manipulation of events and other phenomena. Characters frequently suggest that they are something that they are not in order to suggest to another that he or she is in an entirely different situation than is the case. This is psychological manipulation at a fairly simple level, yet it plays an important role in some works. In the "Verlobung," the most obvious example of this, Gustav is from the beginning an outsider; he seeks a safe environment. The first half of the novella revolves around Babekan's and Toni's attempts to convince him that they represent that haven he seeks. We become very conscious of roles in the novella, not only of deceitful roles which people play in dealing with others, but also of roles of behavior which individuals are taught to play and are expected to play.

In the novella, characters attempt to manipulate behavior patterns of others, and this is most obvious in the leitmotiv of the characters' expecting kindness to be reciprocated by gratitude, and of their expecting good will to be the reward of gratitude. This is obviously a basic dynamic of normal human interaction that ceases, at least in this environment, to be a reliable model for behavior. Babekan uses Gustav's wishful belief in this questionable dynamic to assuage his fears, to deceive and manipulate him, to disarm him literally and figuratively. In order to get Gustav to give up his sword, she cleverly says, "Seid Ihr hereingekommen, um diese Wohltat, nach der Sitte Eurer Landsleute, mit Verräterei zu vergelten?"(164) In this effective, if fairly simple and transparent, manipulation of language and situation, Babekan posits a negative model of behavior, betrayed kindness, in order to elicit its opposite. She suggests the existence of at least a limited environment, her house, where this dynamic of reciprocated kindness functions, and in order for Gustav to receive assistance and enjoy the security he desperately desires, he must demonstrate his wishful faith in that kindness. He shyly gives up his sword and protests his gratitude. In the story which Gustav relates of the young black girl who infects the plantation owner with yellow fever, the grateful plantation owner who has embraced the girl discovers his fatal error in assuming the goodness of the girl's act to be genuine. The failure of this dynamic, though it is of course an example of irony when one considers the duped who expect a certain behavior, does not represent any general Kleistian irony about the expectations of individuals failing to materialize despite the best laid plans. It is a rudimentary form of manipulation that, particularly in this story, is of central importance.

Language is used to create a false environment, and to create an image of oneself that is false, differing from the content underneath. Babekan suggests the settlement is a haven for whites and Creoles. She also subtly creates a definition of herself and Toni that will be reassuring to Gustav. While feigning a condemnation of the revolutionary violence, she casually inserts the information that she and Toni have white blood in them, suggesting they are therefore trustworthy and allies:

> Was kann ich, deren Vater aus St. Jago, von der Insel Cuba war, für den Schimmer von Licht, der auf meinem Antlitz, wenn es Tag wird, erdämmert? Und was kann meine Tochter, die in Europa empfangen und geboren ist, dafür, daß der volle Tag jenes Weltteils von dem ihrigen widerscheint? (165)

She has cleverly picked up the cue from Gustav that he views the matter in simplified terms of black and white, and she replicates the metaphor: as he had said earlier, "Euch kann ich mich anvertrauen; aus der Farbe Eures Gesichts schimmert mir ein Strahl von den meinigen entgegen"(164). Later, Babekan reinforces this suggestion of racial affinity: "um des Europäers, meiner Tochter Vater willen, will ich euch, seinen bedrängten Landsleuten, diese Gefälligkeit erweisen"(167). The we-they breakdown of reality is reinforced(166). The entire conceptual complex of light vs. dark is suggested in her statements, the positive qualities of white vs. the powers of darkness.[8] More ironic for us, and for Babekan, is her willingness to admit to Gustav that she engages in deceit, demonstrating her friendliness by telling Gustav that she deceives the blacks:

> Wenn wir uns nicht durch List und den ganzen Inbegriff jener Künste, die die Notwehr dem Schwachen in die Hände gibt, vor ihrer Verfolgung zu sichern wüßten: der Schatten von Verwandtschaft, der über unsere Gesichter ausgebreitet ist, der, könnt Ihr sicher glauben, tut es nicht!" (165)[9]

In this assurance, which is a kind of toying with Gustav, the motif of the hands makes another appearance, and cunning and deceit is the tool which is placed in the metaphorical hands of those who seek to control others. Where these "hands" operate is in the consciousness of others. She creates the artifice of a small pocket of reality which functions according to rules which do not obtain in the world beyond her door.

Babekan is the conduit of information for Gustav; she controls the sensory input which Gustav receives, and she controls what Gustav can learn of her moral nature and Toni's. Through suggestion, ambiguity, and lies, she creates and modulates the environment into which he has been drawn. He becomes an epistemological prisoner of Babekan, who supplies him with the emotional and perceptual input that effectively renders him immobile and artificially autistic in relationship to the real world. Her sequestering of him in his bedroom facing the courtyard and her locking of doors and shutters is an apt metaphor for the artificiality of the world she suggests and for his quarantine from reality.

The "Verlobung" is a story of inner movements, shifts within the minds of the characters. Gustav's manipulation of Toni is parallel to Babekan's of him. He tries to control her physically and morally, symbolized in his repeated wrapping of his arms around her and his touching of her and grasping her, but the attempt to control her also takes place in the purely verbal arena. The "seduction" of Toni -- already a complicated issue because Gustav also simultaneously seduces himself as he begins to believe his own visions of love which he is attempting to transmit to Toni -- is a manipulation of systems of rules for behavior. The stories he relates to Toni have a specific function in the context of the interaction between Gustav and Toni. First he relates the story of the mock seduction of a plantation owner by the young black woman suffering from yellow fever; and Gustav is hardly unaware of the parallels between the fleeing plantation owner's seeking refuge and his own position at the moment. Next he recalls the story of Mariane's sacrifice and love in the French Revolution. He presents Toni with two models of behavior, two complete systems for defining who one is, how one behaves, what kind of world one can create, and what role one can and ought to play in that world. Complete with commentary and interpretation, these stories are presented to Toni as a kind of moral and existential smorgasbord from which she is to choose who she is and what role she will play.

This is really the aspect of his seduction of her which does work. The sexual advances he makes toward Toni are of lesser import for her, even though Gustav obviously believes that his sexual prowess is what is turning the tide. Her needs are of an entirely different nature. Toni had entered the scene going through the motions of the ruse that Babekan had planned. Toni's motions have precisely the effect on Gustav that Babekan might have wished, but, ironically, her silence, her blushing, her embrace and her weeping, which convince Gustav that she really cares for him, are, it is important to note, really signs of Toni's working through a very different struggle within herself --

that of shame and disenchantment with the very role that she in fact finds herself playing. The real change in Toni occurs when she reacts to the stories which he recounts; she does not at this point react to Gustav directly. She surrenders to him immediately after the tale of Mariane.

The entire novella is remarkable for the way in which completely different systems of reality and meaning stand beside each other without meeting. Individuals who live within the systems do not meet as a result, either, but of course since the characters all have something to conceal, there is no real attempt to appreciate another system. The ambiguity we find so often in Kleist's works -- most densely represented in the Krug and Amphitryon, perhaps -- where utterances mean, and are meant to mean, different things to the listener than to the speaker, where the content of the speaker's mind and soul is consciously concealed, is apparent in this novella as well. Actual points of reference are known only to the speaker. The utterance is valid on two levels and in two systems: the level of transmission and the level of reception are split according to the viewpoint, even though the listener cannot understand the hidden and "real" meaning. Babekan can speak to Gustav of the necessity of deceit and cunning and have him agree with her, for he believes she is talking about deceiving the blacks(165). Thus, when Congo Hoango returns, Toni can point to the bound Gustav and say to Congo Hoango with ostensible pride, "es ist nicht die schlechteste Tat, die ich in meinem Leben getan!"(186) The statement seems to be valid in two different value systems, but it emanates from only

one. Congo _thinks_ she is proud of her act as a demonstration of
loyalty to him and to the revolution; in point of fact she is
loyal to Gustav and to the opposite cause. These are ironies and
ambiguities which the speaker relishes and which the reader can
understand.   It represents a recognition of superiority and
control on the part of the speakers who are toying with the
perceptions, understanding, and knowledge of another person. It
is a part of Kleist's sharp awareness of language as an artificial
construct, bound by the spirit and not by the things, and to which
the spirit is bound. Kleist shows his characters manipulating not
only bits of phenomenal reality, but also language, systems of
meaning, and other people as well.

Kleist attempts to make manifest the relationship between
these things in the interaction between individuals. Much of this
activity does not originate or proceed on the level of emotions or
of personalities.   There is the more basic level of activity to
which Kleist repeatedly draws attention -- that of forming and
transmitting experience.[10] When there is more than one person
involved, and there usually is, there is a skirmish between
freedoms. Kleist's characters have a way of taking note of the
subjectivity of others without taking note of the freedom of
others. The characters exercise their own freedom by manipulating
what others experience -- how they see things, how they view
themselves, how they locate themselves in the framework of a
situation of existence itself.

The process of this manipulation is essentially dishonest; it
involves a deluding of others which seeks to draw the other into a

controlled game which has a particular outcome as a concealed goal. To be sure, a few characters derive at least some amount of enjoyment from playing the game for the mere sake of winning, even though the stakes involved may be of considerable importance to the characters. Strahl in _Käthchen_ clearly enjoys this teasing, if nonetheless damaging, manipulation of others. This is also true of Mercury and Jupiter in the scenes in _Amphitryon_ with Sosias and Amphitryon and of Jupiter in initial scenes with Alkmene. One also notes a similar toying with others in Kunigunde, in Hermann and in the Elector in _Homburg_ who plays with the Prince in the first scene, perhaps more surprisingly, and unconscionably, also in the last scene when the Prince is preparing for death, and in the scene with Natalie when he seems fully aware of the ambiguity of his agreeing to free Homburg; the Elector also stages a minor theatrical coup with his officer corps in the last act when he allows them to expostulate at length on the desirability, even the necessity, of pardoning the Prince, only to then invite the Prince in who announces his decision to accept the death penalty. Most characters, however, are involved in games that are serious games of defending their lives or the unity of their own experience. The basically dishonest activity of this manipulation, as was suggested above, is reflected and frequently incarnated in the deceitful presentation of oneself. How one appears to others is one of the basic elements of the others' experience, for Kleist forces his characters, all of them, to become entangled in the social context; he does not allow them to exist alone.

Chapter 8

THE SOCIAL SELF: THE ACTOR

Underlying the statement that many of Kleist's characters lie and
deceive through the arrangement of their appearance and of their
actions, is the observation that there is a split between the
private and social worlds one inhabits -- between what one thinks
or knows one is and what one is for others. In Kleist criticism
it has gone largely unnoticed how often Kleist's characters are
acting, how often there really _is_ a difference between what
characters are and what they seem to be. It is quite insufficient
to point only to the difficulty Kleist's characters have in
relating to others and knowing others, and it is quite inadequate
to say only that people in his worlds are impenetrable, incapable
of being known. It is not a problem merely of cognition, nor does
it merely lie in the limitations of human nature to be opaque to
others.[1] The characters are frequently impenetrable precisely
because they _choose_ artificiality as a surface with which others
must deal; they _choose_ to erect a facade for themselves and
establish a role which they play to the audience of others. There
is, of course, another side to this problem: some characters have
a role placed on them without their will, as we shall see in
subsequent chapters.

That some of Kleist's characters are not who or what they seem to be, is manifestly clear. The falseness of Kunigunde, or the theft of another's body as in the case of Jupiter's displacing and replacing Amphitryon, or the cheery manipulations and pretences of Hermann, are not isolated examples.[2] Kunigunde's montage of body parts and things to create her appearance, to create what she is for others, is an apt symbolic representation of a similar, though considerably less grotesque and one-sided, activity of characters in many other works. Characters arrange their exterior self as a phenomenal object for the other's experience. The social self which ought to be the mediator between the self and others becomes a manipulated presence that fools and manipulates others as part of the gamesmanship of existing socially and asserting one's autonomy. Many of the characters cast a thin veneer of otherness over themselves while still viewing reality as an extension of their selves, fighting against the freedom of others, avoiding really being a thing in the other's eyes. But while Kunigunde is virtually a schematic representation of this, an abstract metaphor for this theme in Kleist's works, she -- and also Hermann -- are really reduced to that very function of manipulating; that is virtually their sole activity and presence. Somewhat more interesting to the discussion at hand, however, are the characters who are forced into that position by circumstances, who play because in their worlds they play as a matter of course because that is the rule of interaction in that environment or who play because that is what they must do to survive.

In the "Verlobung," for example, Babekan is not the only character who steps outside herself and controls her words and actions for a specific effect on others. Toni and Gustav are each acutely aware of their situations and, from this perspective on their selves and their position, see themselves as causal elements in their contexts, and they consciously order their verbal and physical actions. Gustav is obviously acting in his seduction of Toni, but Toni is not entirely the victim of manipulation in this novella. She, too, plays roles. Since Congo Hoango has tested Toni in cases similar to that of Gustav, it is clear that she has lured men to their deaths repeatedly in the past using her lighter skin color and attractive appearance to draw them into a trap. When she first meets Gustav, her staged epiphany is described thus: "Sie trug Sorge, ... das Licht so zu stellen, daß der volle Strahl davon auf ihr Gesicht fiel"(163). The calculated care, the "so," in her staging of the event is practiced, and it is designed to allay the fears and suspicions of white refugees. This is a role she has been taught to play by Congo Hoango and Babekan, and the skills of deception are an adequate definition of her behavior in nearly all scenes of interaction in the story. She is completely honest with Strömli, but otherwise she follows the exigencies and rules of the environment and dissembles.[3]

Her attempt to save Gustav by arguing openly and rationally with Babekan is aborted almost instantly as she realizes the uselessness of trying to spark sympathy for any white in the mind of Babekan, who, she also does not fail to realize, has the power to destroy both her and Gustav(177f.). Toni employs deception

instead, which is indeed successful. Kleist draws visual attention to Toni's plight, the necessity of erecting a deceptive
facade in this environment where she must keep Gustav uninformed
of her plan and simultaneously prevent Babekan from discovering
her plan: she steps in front of a mirror with a basket of food,
which contains a note to Strömli's band, the key to the success of
her plan. The effective visual image of two Tonis in the room
where both Babekan and Gustav are present underscores her precarious and complicated position as well as her means of handling it.

Toni uses the system of this world, its structures and rules,
to attain her goal. She uses Nanky, the child, as an unwitting
tool to bring Strömli's band to the settlement. The act is
significant because with it she moves to the offensive; her facade
is no longer maintained to preserve a secret but to achieve the
realization of her dream. One must note her manipulation not only
of the system but also of a person -- Nanky. It is, of course, a
sign of the importance of her goal; but it further demonstrates
the pervasive thingness of people as objects to be maneuvered and
the pervasive thingness of oneself when dealing with others. Her
instructions to Nanky -- to be clever, convince them, you will be
rewarded for it -- show her to be a strange role model for the
child. And Nanky will lead them back to the settlement --
"führen," the guiding of people, is a recurring theme in the
story. There is an odd irony for the reader who hears her ask
Nanky, "kann man sich auf dich verlassen?"(182) The expression of
expectation of dependability in a scene of multi-layered deceit
borders on the ridiculous.

Toni's self is split into many facets, and she exists in many spheres: the private reality of their betrothal which must be kept secret, her own perspective on herself as an individual and as a mulatto, her dual role as daughter and adversary of Babekan, the visionary of a future that does not yet exist but which is to be, the agent of machinations to save Gustav and herself, fulfilling Gustav's expectations of her as Mariane. She never loses sight of the physical exigencies of bringing the interplay of these elements to a successful conclusion. The manipulation we have used to describe her earlier actions continues here as Congo Hoango returns, threatening to upset the plans she has already set in motion. The dream and binding scene is parallel to the last act of _Schroffenstein_ where, the male-female roles reversed, Ottokar creates a word-dream for Agnes to hide impending danger from her while disguising her to protect her from that danger. Toni lets Gustav dream while, in order to deceive Congo Hoango and Babekan, she alters the appearance of what is by placing Gustav in the role of prisoner. The manipulation of this appearance of reality, and literal manipulation of Gustav, disrupts the perceptual and cognitive capabilities of every other character present. In her hands she has all the threads of the flow of reality in the story and, with Strömli due to arrive soon, she feels she controls the environment and its direction. She slips back into the role of Congo's ally. Though she is "froh, des Augenblicks mächtig geworden zu sein," it is also her loneliest moment(185). The freedom which she gains by this independence and control is evidence of the perspective she has achieved on others and herself through the moral decision she has made to change her life. Her freedom and her moral stance are bought, of course, with the knowledge that she is excluded, an outsider to everyone, to Congo Hoango and Babekan by her own knowledge and choice, to Gustav by the roles into which she has placed him and herself.

The "Verlobung" is set in an unusual environment that functions according to unusual rules. It is a world of cunning, treachery, and deceit, a world where virtually no one is who or what he seems to be, where even those to whom our sympathy is drawn manipulate, deceive, betray, and kill. It is a world where what an individual sees is more important than what is, where what people are told they see is more important than what they see. It is a world where goodness begets hate and where the reward of kindness is treachery. It is a world of fear. But, one notices, except for the extravagant violence of the historical environment and of the characters' reactions, there are several aspects of the dynamics which are not so unusual in Kleist's works, even those which on the surface seem considerably more placid.

The "Marquise von O...," for example, contains no murders upon the discovery that treachery has occurred, but the Commandant's firing of the pistol into the air suggests that such a tragedy exists there in potential. He "kills" Julietta in a different way, as noted in the earlier, by announcing that he has no daughter any longer, by destroying all evidence of her existence in his world and forbidding her name to be so much as spoken, by trying to erase her from his mind and life. The "Marquise von O...," too, proceeds according to many of the same dynamics as the "Verlobung." As in the "Verlobung" there are secrets kept and guilt over past acts. There is pressure from circumstances that prevents open expression between lover and beloved. There is apparent betrayal and mistakenly placed hatred.

The manipulation of what is, of the rules of behavior, of other people, of one's role, is very much present here as well. But it is largely, though not entirely, concentrated in the character of the Graf. The issue for him, of course, is not physical survival, but his problem is no less important.

As is the case with Gustav in the "Verlobung," the Graf's role-playing and manipulation of others is forced upon him by circumstance. Here, as in Kleist's other works, one has diffi-culty attaching the label of villain to the doers of misdeeds, for characters such as Gustav and the Graf are usually in such dire straits and so much on the defensive that their actions withdraw themselves from the moral judgment of the reader. The truly nefarious deed -- the rape of Julietta -- occupies for this reason an odd position in the novella. What ultimately moves the story is not the act itself but rather the attempt to attach the act or avoid the attachment of the act to a person. The act seems somehow outside the story -- revealed to us only as a printed dash, and our attention as readers is not drawn to the puzzle of who, how, where, and when -- though this puzzle may preoccupy many of the characters themselves. Like the puzzle of Peter's death in Schroffenstein, the act itself here commands our attention less than the reactions of those who must deal with it. The act itself is less important than the complications that arise from the attempt to attach the act to an individual will. And in the end, this act, like that of the "murder" of Peter, becomes the deed that never was. In <u>Schroffenstein</u> the "deed", it turns out, was an uncaused event, not the issue of any human will; here the deed is consciously forgiven at the end of the story and thus "forgotten."

The act is somewhat problematic in two ways. The rape of the Marquise is not described or explicitly mentioned in its chronological place at the beginning of the story. This has the effect of allowing the reader to become acquainted with and consider the Graf's subsequent behavior free of the prejudice of moral disapprobation for the act. As mentioned, the point of the story is to allow us not to judge the morality of the act and thus be forced to define the agent through it, but rather to question that very means of defining a person. The reader, though privy to more information that is pertinent to the Marquise's pregnancy and more aware of clues to the identity of the perpetrator, is almost on the same level of knowledge as the Marquise's family. The narration of the essentials may make it obvious to us that the Graf is responsible for Julietta's pregnancy, but the omission still renders us free to dispassionately observe and explore his subsequent behavior. Along with the Marquise's family, we can view the extraordinary entrance and utterances and actions of the Graf and share and appreciate their bemusement.

Further, the deed presents problems of motivation. It is difficult to integrate it plausibly into the Graf's character since it seems inconsistent with his other acts. As he himself says, this astonishing act is "die einzige nichtswürdige Handlung, die er in seinem Leben begangen hätte"(112). Our response to this problem can be guided by two considerations of consequence to our discussion. Like Peter's death it seems almost an uncaused event, outside the causal pattern of surrounding events; we may view it as the triggering occurrence of the experiment by Kleist, an occurrence which alters the status quo of the environment and of the behavior of his characters as the characters must scramble in reaction to the predicament in which they suddenly find themselves.

Lest one think the act an impossible issue of the Graf's will, however, one ought to note that the selfishness and possessiveness displayed in the rape is apparent in other acts of his as well. The egotistical possessiveness which we see in Gustav, in Amphitryon, and especially in Achilles and Penthesilea is shared by the Graf. At least until the time that Julietta provides him with the opportunity to confess, we see that his vision frequently narrows to his own needs and goals to such an extent that consideration for the feelings and reactions of others is overthrown. His flouting of social form, his inability to take even the most obvious hints and suggestion, his almost abrasive pressure on the Marquise and her family are manifestations of this.

The Graf is in a difficult and complicated situation. His acts in the story are not simple extensions of the self, not examples of spontaneity. Suddenly split into three selves following his act, the Graf is, in some ways, lamed in his choices for action. It is undeniable that he is, first of all, the perpetrator of an immoral and anti-social act. Because this is known only to himself, however, this is a private reality, and his self, as seen by the world, remains intact. These two realities -- the false, or at least incomplete, public image and the hidden dishonourable agent -- are static because they cannot be altered by any outside force.[4]

His problem is the maintenance of his honorable, his good self while coping with the knowledge that such a self ultimately represents a shell which hides the perpetrator of foul deeds. Perhaps most dreadful of all for him is the fact that he himself is at a loss to explain how he could have done such a thing. For him, it is the secret that wants to be let out but which must be concealed. The revelation would provoke the destruction of his good and respected self, his public image which is his social being. One does well to note that it could mean disgrace and death as well, as the executions of the soldiers for attempted rape demonstrates. His compulsion for atonement, therefore, cannot find a solution in confession, the public revelation of the deed. It is true that he seeks death as atonement -- pitching himself feverishly into the thickest of the fight, rolling powder barrels out of burning buildings and the like -- but he sees, as do we, that such an atonement is at root a sham, for it enhances the very public image that is false. His conduct is viewed as exemplary of an imperial officer: it is lauded by his superiors, it strikes the common soldiers with awe, and it fills his foes with admiration. The discrepancy is intensified rather than alleviated, and that night appears to be his finest hour as an officer, as a gentleman, as a human being. The gap between public reality and private reality is physically manifest in his blushing at the praise he receives for his behavior, but the discrepancy remains unknown to others who interpret his silence and blushing as yet another virtue, humility.

The Graf continues to maintain this balancing act, using his good self to cover his bad self. The proposal of marriage, if accepted, will remove his secret shame of the only shameful deed he has committed. It is a kind of cover-up, an attempt to make an honest man of himself. In its essence it is not, at least initially, an atonement but an attempt to make things "all right" without the loss of his reputation. The marriage represents a negation of the act, a denial of the sequence of events. As he says at one point: "daß ... er schon im Begriff sei, die nichtswürdige Handlung wieder gut zu machen"(112). He speaks of a "notwendige Forderung seiner Seele," not of a compelling force of love(111). When he first approaches the Marquise's family with his proposal it is clearly a feeling born of shame, not of giving.

From the beginning until the point where he is granted -- and, with a mixture of gratitude, fear, and courage, decides to take -- the opportunity to confess, the pattern of the Graf's action and appearance is characterized by the presentation of his good self. His dashing rescue of the Marquise establishes an image of himself which he then uses, overuses, and manipulates. In that initial encounter, after driving off the assaulters, he offers the Marquise his arm, "unter einer verbindlichen französischen Anrede" -- a perfect, correct, gallant gesture whose deep effect is not lost on the Marquise who sees him, aside from his gentlemanly performance, as an angel from heaven(195).   His known actions create an extraordinary advantage for him in his subsequent appearances. His next appearance -- apparition, one might say, for into a quiet domestic scene enters the Graf whom all believed dead -- is described in significant terms: "schön, wie ein junger Gott, ein wenig bleich im Gesicht"(110).   That this description refers to the effect on the Marquise is underscored by her first question, "wie er ins Leben erstanden sei?"   At this moment he consciously presses the startling effect of his appearance to advantage for the first time by leaving her in wondrous suspense.   He controls the flow of conversation by not answering her question and instead returning to his own line of questioning which climaxes quickly in his proposal of marriage. This is, in fact, his basic tactic in this scene; he refuses to leave the subject regardless of the bluntest suggestions of the Marquise and her family.

A tension is created between his extremely bad social form in making the proposal and his extraordinarily good social image which allows him many liberties.   He also relies on his record as a much decorated officer, which especially the Commandant must respect and on the obligations which he knows the family must feel.   That these rest on a chimerical footing does not enter into the question because he does not introduce the fact.   He himself tidily sums up his essence for them by giving them the verbal handle by which he wishes to be defined, assuring them, "daß er, mit einem Wort, ein ehrlicher Mann sei"(112). He is defining himself for them, ordering their impressions, trying to control their reactions and perceptions.

In this scene our wonder must center on the Graf's manipulation of the family by capitalizing on their deep sense of obligation, an obligation which he knows is not entirely his due. He asks the family for a favorable response before he departs for Naples -- "wenn irgend etwas in diesem Hause günstig für ihn spreche, -- wobei er die Marquise ansah"(111). Trying to coax support from the Marquise, the person he has in fact most grievously offended, by suggesting her indebtedness to him and the need to demonstrate her gratitude is the moment of greatest irony in the scene, the moment when private world and public posture are most widely asunder.

The remainder of his encounter with the family on this visit is marked by an attempt to control their actions. His announcement that he will ignore his duty and not go to Naples creates a furor of sorts. That he will in fact ignore this duty is clear, but that it represents a bluff of sorts is also likely. Though the family interprets his threat as a bluff, as "Kriegslist," this knowledge does not prevent them from caving in at least partially to his demands; no one "calls" his bluff. We also note that the Graf, like most of Kleist's characters who have an unsavory side, has a good deal of charm. He is expert in creating a good social impression when he desires. He regales the family at table with great skill, shifting his subject matter and style according to the role he uses -- entertaining the father with military matters and stories, the son with hunting matters, chatting with the mother.

The Graf wages a continuing assault on the Marquise. Of the four main encounters between the Graf and the Marquise described in the story, the first three must be considered assaults. The first, of course, a physical assault, the remainder are assaults on her heart and mind. His wondrous appearance in the first scene is echoed in his appearance at her parents' house and then again at her country estate. His wooing has a conscious and controlling air to it, a staginess that is aimed at the Marquise. The shock tactics of his appearance and resurrection when he proposes at her parents' home are repeated at her secluded estate where she believes herself to be in isolation. Sneaking through an open gate into her garden behind the house he stealthily approaches her and, once again, appears to her.[5] That he consciously creates his "sudden appearance" is obvious to the reader: "Er näherte sich ihr so, daß sie ihn nicht früher erblicken konnte, als bis er am Eingang der Laube, drei kleine Schritte von ihren Füßen, stand" (128). The involved structure of the sentence describes the purposeful manner of his approach, the "so", while the final, separated verb, "stand", shows the result, the sudden effect of his efforts. He appears before her standing, motionless, smiling, and remains standing motionless for a while before approaching her person.[6]

The Graf strives to convey to her the sentiment that he is somehow larger than life, that he is somehow more than a mere suitor, that his love for her and his motivation for marrying her

are greater and more compelling than the love and the relationships of normal people. He intimates that he and his love for her
are on a higher plane. He presents himself as the knower of
innocence and of secrets, convinced of her innocence, disdainful
of the woefully limited judgment rendered by her family and by the
world. He says, "als ob ich allwissend wäre, als ob meine Seele
in deiner Brust wohnte"(129). The mysterious light in which he
appears to her in both scenes is calculated to enhance her image
of him. In this scene he casts himself as the gentle bearer of
comfort, as the lover who will elevate her above the charges and
recriminations of the world, as the restorer of innocence, as the
rock to which she can cling in her distress. He creates the
impression that the mysterious comfort he brings is commensurate
with the amazing predicament in which she finds herself. He
offers, in short, to remove her from that world and provide her
with sanctuary, to take her into his private world in which everything is all right. He offers to save her. What he does not yet
offer her, however, is the truth. Rather, his approach in this
encounter indicates that he seeks the perpetuation of his secret.
He offers to save her, but he also seeks to be saved himself.

The range of ways in which Kleist's characters play roles and
manipulate others through acting is obviously very broad. The
mechanism is clearly quite similar in the cases of Hermann,
Kunigunde, Toni, Gustav, and the Graf, but the motivations vary
enormously. This is obvious when one considers the emphasis that
Kleist places on the dependence of the social self on other
characters. The role-playing manipulating characters come to

interpret what they ought to be from what other characters tell them they ought to be. The role-players fit themselves into other people's system of expectations and from that position order their exterior appearances and actions. Here one notices the differences between the role-players and the victims. The adaptability of the role-player has nothing to do with the adaptability of someone like Sylvester. Sylvester adapts, to be sure, to an entirely new system of reality, but he retains nothing that really is of _his_ world; he capitulates, in essence. The characters discussed in this chapter retain their freedom behind the artifice of their acts and appearances. They set out to win the battle for what is to be.

In these cases of role-playing, the actor is cognizant of the subjectivity of the other but toys with it and relegates it to a level which is taken less seriously than it morally ought to be if true interaction were to be the goal. When Achilles, as a final example in this argument, sets out to be "defeated" by Penthesilea, he reveals the part of his nature that is, or has become, the cavalier actor. His gesture, though he _does_ love Penthesilea, is not really the sacrifice that it may seem at first glance: he is not really giving up everything of value in order to follow her. His act is far more an expression of his own freedom; he tries to stand free outside his own Greek world and outside the world of love with Penthesilea. It is a disastrous maneuver for him, of course, because he goes about it in an overconfident fashion. He overestimates the extent to which he _can_ stand free and outside these two contexts. Kleist's Achilles, unlike Homer's

Achilles, does not withdraw from the battle for basically "Greek" reasons, wounded honor and pride. He withdraws because it simply ceases to be an important thing to do. He reveals that it really is just one of the roles that he plays. Odysseus, of course, is outraged, and he says quite accurately and perceptively of Achilles:

> Und unseren Helenenstreit,
> Vor der Dardanerberg, der Sinnentblößte,
> Den will er, wie ein Kinderspiel, weil sich
> Was anders Buntes zeigt, im Stiche lassen? (2907-10)

The Greeks are perplexed because they are warriors in the Trojan War, and that Achilles can simply walk off and leave the ten-year long national war behind him, forgetting it "like a daydream," is virtually inconceivable to them(2517). Achilles indeed walks off, leaving behind his "costume," the bronze armor, a gift from Thetis.[7]

Achilles also walks off to join Penthesilea with the same illusion that he can simply play a game there, too. He is not capitulating to Penthesilea; he is appearing to surrender his freedom in order that he might win her. In his own mind he is retaining complete control over what he is and what he is doing, and over Penthesilea. He talks of following Penthesilea to Themiscyra for a month, possibly two or three at the most -- he retains the right to improvise -- but he still thinks of bringing her back and setting her on the throne: she is still more object than subject for him. He protests that he wants to see the temple of Diana at Penthesilea's home(2530); but he imagines that he can simply build a replica of such a temple for her in his own land

(2292). He misjudges Penthesilea badly here when he believes he can transport her to a new stage setting and satisfy the needs of her soul.

Achilles entirely misses the fact that Penthesilea is quite the opposite of him; she puts her entire being into her roles; it is not a game for her, and she has not any of the freedom of distance which characterizes his standpoint. Achilles unfortunately projects a portion of his attitude onto her, however, and he finds it marvelously "well done," albeit with some doubts, when he learns that Penthesilea is approaching the duel with a full battle train, replete with riders, hounds and elephants: "Gut. Dem Gebrauch war sie das schuldig. Folgt mir. -- O sie ist listig, bei den ewigen Göttern!"(2540-1) His arrogance is loaded with tragic irony: he announces that the battle hounds are as tame as she is. He is right, of course, but he errs when he thinks that he controls her as a tamed animal. That he believes the hounds would eat out of his hand, just as he imagines he has got Penthesilea to do, is particularly ironic from the reader's standpoint considering the fate which awaits him when he meets Penthesilea and her hounds. In an entirely unanticipated way, he does become the victim in the drama he set in motion.[8]

Part of Achilles' problem is that he makes an assumption that Penthesilea exists, or can exist, partly as conscious facade. But that sort of interaction brings problems of its own. The manipulation of one's social self is so common an occurrence and theme in Kleist's works that the mechanics of such interactions and the effect of two facades meeting, must be considered separately.

Chapter 9

FACADE AND INTERACTION

So many characters exist socially as artifice that one is tempted
to think of the environments in Kleist's works as representing the
world as theater. But it is at times an undramatic sort of drama
which is played out: few of the players share the same script.
Role-players are frequently trying to maneuver others into playing
a specific part in the scenario he or she has in mind, and often
they succeed, at least in the short run. Those characters who are
capable of being manipulated obviously want to believe the good
they see in others and the good they see in their relationships
with others, but trust and faith in other people seems to be a
very expensive quality emotionally for many of Kleist's characters. Regardless of whether such characters arrive at suspicions of others correctly or not, if they sense at all that the
expectations they had of another person have not been met or have
not been reciprocated, or if they sense their faith in another was
misplaced, the reaction is swift and terrible. The opening of the
self to another in caring or in trust, whether justifiably done or
not, represents an enormous investment of what the characters are,
an investment which is made with apprehension, one is led to
believe, because of the vulnerability these characters expose.

Characters will continue to believe in others, not least of all because they are placing faith in their own faith as much as they are placing faith in the other person, and they can be slow in realizing that they are being fooled. But faith in others crumbles at the slightest doubt. Almost predictably, characters will believe instantly that others are dissembling and lying. The speed with which others are condemned for duplicity is striking. In the "Marquise," the Commandant banishes his daughter from the house within minutes of hearing a report of her pregnancy; he takes the report as the truth and does not so much as ask his daughter whether the report is true, much less seek an explanation of the circumstances and facts from her own mouth. Similarly, when Eve is seen with "someone," neither Frau Marthe nor Ruprecht ask such questions as, "what is the meaning of this?" or, "how long has this been going on?" The same can be said of the reactions of Littegarde's brothers in the "Zweikampf." There is an immediate acceptance that the appearance of a single incident indicates duplicity and that that duplicity is a sign of complete moral rot. It is small wonder that the Graf is reluctant to freely confess his crime.

Evil in others is very credible to characters in Kleist's worlds, while goodness is suspect. If it is not disease and death which fester beneath a surface of kindness and love, as in the case of the young woman who infects the plantation owner seeking aid in the "Verlobung," then it is at least a private world that is an affront to others precisely because it is hidden -- and, more importantly, because it is lied about. If there is one thing that Kleist's characters seem to hate more than anything else, it is being fooled. That cuts to a deeper level than anger at not being told the truth: it seems to hit them near the core of their being; the feeling that they have been used sends Kleist's characters into rage, not wounded sadness. It is, after all, not Julietta's pregnancy, or even the suspicion that Julietta has had a secret love affair, that leads to the mother's outrage against her daughter. Rather, it is the suspicion that Julietta is manipulating her, exploiting her maternal trust and gullibility to avoid censure and revelation of a secret life. That crime is unforgivable. Julietta's father is even more enraged at what he takes to be Julietta's duplicity which he describes as diabolical. This is the same rage of Gustav against Toni, of Thusnelda against Ventidius, of Penthesilea against Achilles.

Characters also react to others' trying to manipulate them verbally. There is knowledge that language can be used to create a facade behind which a hidden and different reality of evil intent lurks. Characters are aware of the power of the word, and they are also aware that others use and manipulate people through the word. The mistrust of the word makes them sensitive to the lie. In Schroffenstein, a play very much about lies and manipulation, Jeronimus, after hearing Rupert's harangue at the beginning of the first scene, rejects the elaborate metaphor Rupert has created, and he rejects the declaration of the war of destruction. "Ich habe hier in diesen Bänken wie ein Narr gestanden, dem ein Schwarzkünstler Faxen vormacht," he says (106-8). The language and the artificial reality the language

creates are rejected as a conscious construct, as verbal sleight
of hand, as illusion. Jeronimus also has occasion to accuse
Sylvester of the same thing: "O du Quacksalber der Natur! Denkst
du, ich werde dein verfälschstes Herz auf Treu und Glauben zweimal
als ein echtes kaufen?"(673-5)

The tool of manipulation here is language, something shifted
and arranged in order to shift and arrange what others know and
believe. It stops being a means of explanation and becomes a
thing, a tool to manipulate others. The thingness of the words is
related to a thingness of the stuff of reality, alterable and able
to be manipulated in the minds of others. Indeed, words are
referred to as things within the play. Ottokar bursts out at
Jeronimus: "O du Falschmünzer der Gefühle! Nicht einen wird ihr
blanker Schein betrügen; am Klange werden sie es hören, an die Tür
zur Warnung deine Worte nageln"(143-6). It is people, though,
that are the true objects of manipulation in these cases. The
resistance to being manipulated is fierce if the attempt is
recognized. In the same play, Johann violently repulses such an
attempt by Ottokar:

> Du Tor! Du Tor! Denkst du mich so zu fassen?
> Weil ich mich edel nicht erweise, nicht
> Erweisen will, machst du mir weis, ich seis,
> Damit die unverdiente Ehre mich
> Bewegen soll, in ihrem Sinn zu handeln?
> Vor deine Füße werf ich deine Achtung. (835-40)

Johann recognizes the unreality, the thingness of Ottokar's
construct, and treats it appropriately, calling the abstract value
a thing which he hurls back at its creator. It is not only the
lying with words which is at issue here; it is also the lying with

one's actions, the role-playing, which arouses such mistrust and suspicion. The characters in Schroffenstein, almost to a person, expect actions to be insincere. When a traveller reports the death of the herald to Rupert, he uses a very telling formula to explain Sylvester's role in the murder: "er tat, als wüßt ers nicht, und ließ sich bei der Tat nicht sehen"(1535-6, emphasis mine). Aside from the fact that the traveller obviously believes Sylvester engineered the murder, the very formulation of his accusation belies Sylvester's absence from the scene. The juxtaposition of the "act" of not being there with the act of murder linguistically connects the two phenomena, one of which is in fact not a phenomenon at all.

The failure of Sylvester to appear at the scene is made out to be a conscious act of creating a facade of non-involvement. Sylvester's subsequent chiding of the agents is also seen as an assumed role, perhaps even by the agents themselves, whom he nearly simultaneously calls his faithful vassals. The whole incident of the herald's murder has a great effect on the action of the play, primarily because of the perceived falseness of Sylvester's actions, that is, his feigning to fall into unconsciousness before Aldöbern is killed. Rupert's fury at the incident, and the artifice of Sylvester, prompts his toying with Jeronimus; he believes he is reacting to Jeronimus according to exactly the same model used by Sylvester:

```
Rupert:              Bist du denn ein Herold? -- ?
Jeronimus: Dein Gast bin ich, ich wiederhols. --Und wenn
       Der Herold dir nicht heilig ist, so wirds
       Der Gast dir sein.
Rupert:              Mir heilig? Ja. Doch fall
       Ich leicht in Ohnmacht. (1781-4)
```

In this encounter Jeronimus chooses a very bad strategy. He feigns agreement with Rupert in order to try to alter Rupert's plans. In his fatal journey to Rossitz to arrange a meeting between Sylvester and Rupert, Jeronimus pretends to align himself with Rupert, and, having established a pattern of thought parallel to that of Rupert, he hopes to guide Rupert's thoughts away from vengeance long enough for the two brothers to meet. His feigned agreement, alas, is too transparent. "Allein, trotz allem, der Verdacht bleibt groß, und fast unmöglich scheints -- zum wenigsten sehr schwer, doch sich davon zu reinigen," Jeronimus says in a pretense of suspecting Sylvester(1727-30). The combination of disinterest and sympathy is seen instantly as a ruse, for aside from the fact that Jeronimus is not very convincing, Rupert already has news that Jeronimus killed Johann. Rupert meets ruse with ruse and plays along, only appearing to agree to a meeting with Sylvester.

Jeronimus is playing a dangerous game, and he is singularly unequipped to handle the intensely powerful wills around him. He had already been placed firmly in Warwand's camp because of his attachment to Agnes; he has, as Rossitz has heard, slain Johann; and then he arrives with a message from Sylvester, who has, Rupert believes, just had the messenger from Rossitz killed. He adopts precisely the wrong ploy when he pretends a viewpoint that is not true, for it is precisely the duplicity of Sylvester that is the current source of Rupert's ire. And Jeronimus' reference to Sylvester's appearance of goodness seems almost calculated to anger Rupert: "Ein einzger Blick auf sein ehrwürdig Haupt, hat schnell das Wahre mich gelehrt"(1748-9).

Meeting a facade with a facade of one's own is not unusual, though perhaps sometimes a bit surprising. In the "Marquise," the mother's anger at being deceived does not prevent her from approaching Julietta in a similar fashion. In the desire to make her daughter "reveal her soul," the mother fabricates a story, feigns an apology for casting Julietta from the family, lies that she and the Commandant are convinced of her innocence, and creates a mythical rapist and reports his confession. There is clearly an ironic quality to the idea of having a ruse result in the removal of a suspected ruse and in the joyous revelation of truth. It is not the only time this happens, however. In the "Verlobung," Toni, who loathes the lie she has been living, uses deception and lies and manipulation in her dealings with every other character in the story save Strömli, yet she brings about a state of affairs where all deceptions are revealed.

A similar situation occurs between Ottokar and Agnes in act III, scene 1 of Schroffenstein, the "poisoning scene." Agnes is aware who Ottokar is and knows that he has sworn to kill her. He knows who she is, but he believes her to be ignorant of his identity. He is manipulating her here by leaving her in ignorance of this most important fact, but we must grant that his reasons are quite sound, for he fears to lose her if she discovers his identity. However, it is really Agnes who has the upper hand here as far as knowledge is concerned, and she plays the scene holding him in ignorance of her own knowledge. She begins an unusual experiment, inserting herself into a game. She does not confront him with his supposed unrevealed identity until after she has drunk from his hands what she believes, or at least strongly fears, to be poison. She is conducting a test of Ottokar and of the situation, and she is the subject of the experiment as well.

In this scene the breakthrough in the ring of distrust occurs. It is paradoxical that it comes to pass not out of trust but out of the creation of a facade. This facade is the conscious maintenance of innocence and ignorance in the face of Ottokar's own facade, i.e. a facade that is identical with no facade at all. Ottokar mistakes it for trust in him, but the result is the same. She appears to be guileless by being a victim consciously. Her wish is that Ottokar means her no harm, and she is the subject of her own experiment to find out whether that can be true. By laying her life on the line in the experiment, she brings about precisely the reality she wishes were true. This is not cunning on her part but partly exhaustion and partly an unwillingness to continue the situation in which fear chokes the possibility of love.

Artifice meeting artifice is not uncommon in Kleist's works, but the outcomes are seldom as felicitous as this scene where the duality of perceptions is reintegrated into a unified perception of reality, the rare occurrence of a shared experience, after a game of facades. Kleist's characters place such a high premium on form and stability that one frequently realizes that the form of a character's life, the social self, is empty and role-like. There is a slight suggestion of this in the "Marquise von O...," though

it does not begin to compare with the "Findling." The world of
the "Marquise," though it develops into a world of clashing needs
and personalities, initially seems to present no problems. The
microcosm of the Marquise's family rests on a framework of econ-
omic, social, personal, and ethical values and norms which do not
strike us as unusual. It is not a framework which is ossified
into pure form without substance, for in it flourish a certain
harmony and love -- parental, filial, conjugal. Undisturbed, it
remains a workable model.

Nevertheless, the forms have taken on a certain life of their
own, and this microcosm threatens to become exclusive and
inflexible. At the center of this world, and of the story, is the
family, closed unto itself. The framework of values is so
entrenched and orderly in this family that a certain personal
dimension is lost, or at least obscured. Certain values are taken
for granted and form takes their place. Though we sense at the
beginning and later discover that affections in the family are
deep, we hear little actual exchange of affection or expression of
concern for daily personal matters. The language the family
members use is stylized and formal; problems are avoided in
discussion, as was noted in the preceding chapter; the order is
defended, the status quo upheld. When something upsets the order,
it is resisted, as in the case of the Graf, or it is removed.
Julietta violates the familial roles and appears to have betrayed
the love and trust of the family; the parents recoil from her as
much as they push her away from themselves. They retreat to the
family mold again, but they retain a hollow and incomplete form

that is devoid of substance. There is a certain degree of role-playing involved in being a family member in that household, but it hardly represents the core of the story as it does in the "Findling."

The environment of the "Findling" is bleak, cold, and sterile. It is not a world whose social order is in upheaval or in a state of collapse; it is a world whose social form is frozen into a tableau devoid of meaning. Such concepts as son, parents, family, wife, husband, and marriage are shells which contain nothing of the bonds of love which underlie these forms in the Marquise's family. Unlike the apparent seeking for affection and security in "Verlobung," the characters here, locked unto themselves in seething private worlds of longing, frustration, guilt, selfishness, and feelings of inferiority, carry on a masquerade that intensifies their own loneliness and saps the others of hope and of any remnants of love.[1] The forms are hollow, where facades are erected to cover secret worlds, veritable abysses that belie the calm surface and in which evil festers. The forms are so frozen, the private worlds so hidden, that a tableau of family life is at the center of the stage upon which nothing happens while everything of import occurs offstage in the private worlds.

The characters lead separate private lives while maintaining the form of a family. Piachi occasionally "checks" on Elvire; Nicolo lives in separate apartments; the house seems filled with doors behind which the characters live. People knock at doors, listen at doors, peak through keyholes; doors are closed, they are locked; people carry keys for doors. The doors symbolize the barrier between public image and the private world, the barrier which hides what they are. There is a static quality to the public forms: the marriage between Piachi and Elvire does not represent a union of souls; the motion which speech and conversation would supply to the relationship is largely missing. For example, the narrator describes no commiseration or exchange between Piachi and Elvire when Piachi reports the death of Paolo: their grief seems private. Piachi and Elvire and Nicolo sit silently for long periods when they find themselves together in the public areas of the house. The silence is, by the time the story has progressed midway, quite suffocating. This is not a mere lack of conversation; there is nothing there to support it.[2]

That Nicolo is a person of facade cannot be questioned, but despite the vehemence with which the narrator denounces him, we find it difficult to view him simply as evil. He grows up confronted with unhealthy role models which have an unfortunate effect on the formation of his character. His step-parents do not live openly; it is a house of secrets. We surmise from his almost pathological fear of disapproval that his upbringing was not only stern but was structured so as to mold him into rigid types of behavior. When Elvire falls, for example, we read, "Da das Geräusch, das sie gemacht hatte, notwendig den Alten herbeiziehen mußte, so unterdrückte die Besorgnis, einen Verweis von ihm zu erhalten alle andere Rücksichten ..."(204). He disappears quickly. The need to **appear** good actually reduces the dimension of humanity in him.[3]

For Nicolo, and for many of the other characters discussed in this chapter, the issue was one of freedom -- freedom for oneself or freedom from something. The reader is continually made aware of the contingency of individuals on others and of the dependence of rules of behavior on others. The stories frequently consist of clashes between freedoms. Thus, while reality is relativized by individuals, individuals also find themselves put in danger of losing control over their own world. Kleist forces his characters to be involved with the world, though clearly some of them would just as soon retreat from all contexts and from all contact, and avoid the risk of living; they exhibit an almost primal fear of involvement with the world and with others. Some of the characters become involved only insofar as they play a role. And the Kleistian question arises repeatedly: how can one exist and be oneself under these circumstances? Just what is underneath the social self, the role that ought to mediate between one's inner self and the world outside, is a question that clearly preoccupies Kleist. He indeed poses the question of what happens when individuals must confront the way they are contingent on others, of what happens when they ask the question of who they themselves are.

Chapter 10

PRIVATE WORLDS AND IDENTITY

Existing in Kleist's worlds is a difficult task, not least of all,
as the preceding chapter demonstrated, because the most basic
aspect of the characters' environment -- other people --
frequently turns out to be unreliable artifice. But Kleist's
characters are not evil, and one searches in vain for true
villains in Kleist's works.[1] The facades which so many characters
present as their social selves cover a great deal that goes on
underneath. It is useless to say that Kleist's characters ought
to act more truthfully, for they are often forced into the roles
they feel they must play.[2] Kleist's characters are afraid to open
themselves to others, and the reasons for this vary along a scale
ranging from the purely practical exigencies of the situation to
an inherent fear on the level of participation in life in general.
In any case, the mere presence of so much role-playing -- and its
frequency -- demands an examination of the content and nature of
the self that is hidden from view. There is a tension in Kleist's
works between private worlds and public roles, between what
characters know and what they say, between what they think they
are and how they present who they are, at times between attempted
solipsism and existence itself.

Kleist's characters spend a great deal of time out of direct touch with the real world which surrounds them, and this has been viewed by some critics as a virtue, of course. Curt Hohoff, for example, believes that the only condition in which the _true_ person appears is in withdrawal, in unconsciousness, in the dream, and that the only true order is a transcendental order.[3] Such a description is based, obviously, on a value distinction between the social world -- the world where one establishes an existence and an identity for oneself and for others -- and a posited world apart from and above that social world, where some transcendental essence exists. What the first two chapters of this study have sought to demonstrate, however, is that the world of the mind of Kleist's characters is not fundamentally one of absolute or transcendental truths, but rather frequently one of fundamental dishonesty -- dishonesty with oneself and with one's own experience as well as dishonesty with others. By establishing a tension between "real" reality and a transcendental reality, Hohoff and others bypass what is basically an enormous tension on a different level. When one defines the tension as existing between reality and transcendence, one ends up fashioning terms that are paradoxical and inappropriate to Kleist's work. Fricke, for example, tries to bridge the two realms he posits as the poles of this tension, with the term "ewig-konkrete Bestimmung" -- the individual's unique and timeless essence which attempts to realize itself in the phenomenal world -- which Fricke sees as the sacred goal of Kleist's characters.[4] One does better to note the tension on the psychological level, between characters and especially within characters themselves. It rests on a discrepancy between where characters exist in their own minds and how they exist and come to terms with the roles they find themselves playing in social contexts.

The private worlds that Kleist's characters exist in are indeed likely to be outside of space and time, but transcendence implies a location that is misplaced for what the characters are actually experiencing. The reason the reality in which they exist does not coincide with what is going on about them, as was argued earlier, is that these characters evade and deny what surrounds them. They frequently retreat from important aspects of their environment or from the environment itself and do not come to a knowledge of their selves; they sidestep the reality around them by not confronting it at all or by altering their experience of it. As stated above, the reasons for this retreat vary greatly among the contexts which Kleist supplies in his works, but the mechanism is much the same.

Hidden in, or sometimes locked into, private worlds behind social facades, the characters encounter things and events around them on such a level of distortion, and they interact with others with such skewed engagement, that it becomes necessary to qualify the assertion that they exist in the real world at all. In the "Verlobung," Gustav's relationships to his environment and to Toni do not represent any genuine encounter between Gustav and what lies outside him. We have already noted the way in which Gustav, confronted with extraordinary circumstances, bypasses the wretched environment of the present by retreating to recall of a lost past, to anticipations of a wished-for future, and to dreams. He does everything in his power to prevent a realization of the present by existing out of time in mental constructs. He hardly encounters Toni, either, for he comes to wishfully experience her as the embodiment of an idealized recollection of Mariane. His entire private reality is a system of fantasies and illusions.

What makes Gustav's illusion so interesting in the story is that it becomes as real as it does: Toni accepts the role that Gustav assigns to her, and she begins to share his private world of illusions. After the scene in which their tears mix and, between paragraphs, they make love, Toni models her actions on the actions of Mariane which Gustav has narrated to her. Even after Gustav glares at her with hatred and contempt when he thinks she has bound him for surrender to Hoango, she experiences a certain rejoicing at the possibility of achieving total fulfillment of the role by perishing while saving Gustav:

> ... es mischte sich ein Gefühl heißer Bitterkeit in ihre Liebe zu ihm, und sie frohlockte bei dem Gedanken, in dieser zu seiner Rettung angeordneten Unternehmung zu sterben. (187)

She derives a certain comfort from fantasizing on her own nobility, and there is also a suggestion of pride in having proved the equal of Mariane when she strolls into the room on the arm of Strömli near the end of the story.

The love between Toni and Gustav rests on a chimerical footing, indeed. Gustav's private world does not incorporate Toni as a person; he has a conception of Toni that is flat and lacks differentiation. Further, given his black-and-white ordering of

all elements in this environment, we realize that he transforms
her into a white rather than noting and accepting the necessity
for differentiation in her person and rather than accepting the
complexity of her personality and of her position in Haiti -- as
Babekan's daughter, as a mulatto, as a non-European, as a protegee
of Congo Hoango, as an individual who is herself trapped,
defensive, and in need of being saved. Gustav loves Mariane, not
Toni, and for her part, she does not love Gustav so much as she
loves the man who loved Mariane and whom Mariane loved. Their
point of coincidence in love originates in, and to a large extent
is based on, the private memory of Mariane's love; they love each
other by proxy.

Beyond the mirage of its fulfillment their love has some
further weakness in its concrete foundations. It should be noted
that as lovers and beloveds they "meet" only three times, aside
from the encounter when he murders her. The nature of these
meetings fits the pattern of private worlds' missing each other
that has been developed in other ways. In the first meeting,
which, like the others, is really a non-meeting, they have set out
to seduce each other and both begin by playing deceptive roles.
Gustav tries to seduce Toni by creating a facade of tender care
while manipulating her to secure information and her loyalty. In
the same scene, which Toni initiates by also playing a deceptive
role, she weeps and is silent, occupied with her own unexpressed
thoughts and feelings, while Gustav protests his love to the
illusory Mariane-Toni. After making love she falls asleep. It is
while she is thus unconscious that Gustav carries her to her bed

"wie eine Leblose," caresses her, calls her his bride once again, kisses her and rushes back to his room(176). Like many scenes in this novella, in this meeting gestures carry the action more than words.

The characteristic tendency of the novella genre to rely heavily on dramatic gesture is particularly apparent in the "Verlobung" and effectively reinforces here the theme of "communication" that occurrs to a large extent as an individual's private experience and assumptions rather than as a sharing of what characters know or of what they are. Of the times Gustav and Toni are together, the most tender expressions of their love occur without words, each of them immersed in dreams of an idyllic future -- dreams which are a pastiche of lovers' traditional hopes; dreams which, like the dreams of Jeronimus and Josephe or of Ottokar and Agnes, will not be allowed to materialize. In silent embrace with Toni after he has convinced himself that she represents no threat, Gustav inhales her sweet breath(173). And likewise when Toni later goes to Gustav in the scene which is a mirror reflection of that, she comes to him while he is asleep, unconscious, dreaming, and she bends over him, caresses him, calls him by his name while inhaling his sweet breath, and kisses him(183f.). Without saying another word to him, she hears the return of Congo: she binds him, kisses him again and rushes to meet Congo Hoango. Her tenderness while he is asleep is, significantly, the only time she calls him by his name in the story, and he misses it. Ironic for us is Toni's well-meaning decision not to awaken him, talk with him and tell him everything about herself. By leaving him in a _dream_ of her rather than speaking with him with honesty, she helps bring on the final catastrophe. In the peculiar dynamic which develops between and around them, they love intensely without ever really meeting each other, and there is a final pathetic irony in the way that Gustav can say, after murdering her, "du warst mir durch einen Eidschwur verlobt, obschon wir keine Worte darüber gewechselt hatten!"(193)

These two scenes of non-interaction between characters locked within their own private concerns frame the only other meeting between them. This takes place in the real world, one might say, for Babekan is present. Gustav puts his arm around Toni, asks her how she slept and also asks, in his ignorance of the true state of affairs, whether he should tell Babekan about their betrothal. Toni is understandably horrified at the suggestion: she removes herself from his arm and says, "wenn Ihr mich liebt, kein Wort!" and she leaves the room(181). She obviously must forbid the public verbal expression of this love which is clearly not capable of surviving in the real world. Even their "collusion" in the creation of the phantom relationship based on the dead Mariane is played out separately, because their own private worlds incor- porate Mariane in two very different ways, ways that are not shared and are not allowed to be shared.

Gustav and Toni are forced into a full retreat from the world, at least in the way they enter and live in their private realities; it is as much the bizarre nature of the betrothal as its tragic outcome that makes it the novella's unheard-of occurrence. The final image of the novella, a monument erected by

Strömli to Gustav and to Gustav's betrothed, "die treue Toni," is as completely ironic to us as any other thing which the characters do(195). It is a monument to a betrothal that never really esisted, artificially uniting Gustav and Toni in a lifeless eternal embrace. It also freezes them into the same sort of static and lifeless image that was the problem of the relationships in the story. Replacing Gustav's bloodless image of a "faithful Mariane" with a bloodless image of a "faithful Toni" is a final insult to her humanity.

This novella is not, however, the only time in Kleist's works when marriages or attempts at marriages are based on the shakiness of a tension between private worlds and social context. It is equally true of the Graf's proposal of marriage in the "Marquise von O..." and of the marriage between Piachi and Elvire in the "Findling."

The Graf ends up in the situation of being the only one to know of his crime. His secret is a reality of which only he is aware, but even he has difficulty in admitting it to himself. On one level he is quite conscious of the way in which he attempts to prevent the revelation of his secret and to maneuver the Marquise and her family into the marriage. On another level, however, his motivations do not appear to be quite so simple. Without doubting the sincerity of his desire to marry the Marquise, one nevertheless wonders at his early monomaniacal fixation on the marriage itself as an institution. His exasperation upon hearing of Julietta's expulsion and exile is in perfect harmony with his fixation: "Wenn die Vermählung erfolgt wäre: so wäre alle

Schmach und jedes Unglück uns erspart!"(128) And, like this wish, it is precisely in the subjunctive mode that he goes about living in the story until he finds release in his decision to confess. At this point his vision is aimed at marriage as a problem-free idyllic retreat where his crime somehow will no longer have social import. The narrowness and unreality of his vision preclude any insight into the difficulties which would have arisen in any case if she had accepted his proposal of marriage when he first asked -- difficulties arising from the subsequent birth of the child and, more to the point, from the reaction of the Marquise to the confession he would of necessity then have had to make if the marriage were a fait accompli. Although this is not damning evidence of a cavalier attitude towards the whole affair, his seeming lack of concern for the latter problem is a result of his myopically planned goals and actions at this point and of his tenuous contact with reality and of his fear.

In the garden scene which was discussed in the preceding chapter, the Graf presents himself to Julietta as the representative of a firm love and trust to which she can cling though her own world has crumbled about her. The irony of this scene lies in the fact that, although the Marquise is herself in retreat and has shut herself off from the real world, she has come to terms with her predicament and has a much better grasp on herself and on reality than he. She has just decided to reenter the real world when he arrives with his most inopportune and inappropriate of suggestions. His desire to seal himself up with her within the walls of the minimal world in which he believes she is living and his suggestion to ignore the significance of child, family, and world, are in a different place and time from where and when she now exists. He is attempting to woo her into an artificial and lost world created in his mind. He seems to offer her his private and safe world of selfless love, but in fact he tries to embrace and enter her private world, a world she is in the process of leaving. For him it is a world away from the judging eyes of community, where he imagines he could live alone with her and remain intact in the confines of their love. The boundary here between the Graf's self-delusion and his deluding of Julietta is impossible to locate.

In the "Findling," all of the main characters actually spend more of their time in the worlds they live in behind their social facades than they do interacting with others around them. It is the private world of Elvire that is the center of the story. It is the world which Piachi cannot break into and the world Nicolo tries to enter forcibly. Elvire's physical presence is so intangible precisely because she really exists in another time and another place and lives with a person who no longer exists. It is the central moral irony of the novella that from the existence of a private world composed of love, gratitude, and caring arises a poisoning of the real environment. She is really alive only in this private world. Her emotionless and blank face in public is replaced by emotion and humanity in private. And it is to this humanness that Nicolo reacts and to which he is drawn when he discovers the existence of a hidden Elvire.

There is a similarity between Nicolo and Elvire that becomes obvious not only to us but to Nicolo as well. They both are turned inward and both have expressionless faces which betoken a private life hidden by a shell. Nicolo's instinctive belief, based on the knowledge of his own posturing, that Elvire must lead another life behind the flawless but cold exterior proves quite correct. Elvire may well sense this affinity also. She does not, after all, reveal her discovery of Xaviera's maid in Nicolo's room; she keeps it a secret. And the incident is the only time, other than when she is "with" Colino, that we see the normally hidden emotions. It is the point when Nicolo for the first time consciously considers the possibility of her hidden world:

> Der Unwille, der sich mit sanfter Glut auf ihren Wangen entzündete, goß einen unendlichen Reiz über ihr mildes, von Affekten nur selten bewegtes Antlitz; es schien ihm unglaublich, daß sie ... nicht selbst zuweilen auf dem Wege wandeln sollte, dessen Blumen zu brechen er eben so schmählich von ihr gestraft worden war. (206)

While Nicolo maintains that he wishes to unmask Elvire and reveal her dissembling, he actually attempts to do something different and considerably less public. He intends to enter her private world rather than destroy it. He dons the role of her "lover" in order to gain admittance. She faints, of course, and he intends to rape her if need be, but he places her on the bed to revive her. Unlike the Graf's rape of the Marquise, this rape is not meant to be hidden, but to be shared by them. Though hardly for Elvire, whose private world and, indeed, whose life are destroyed by Nicolo's sullying intrusion, the "fulfillment" for

Nicolo comes from the merging of their private worlds, if only in an encounter he does not expect to repeat.

It is a peculiar sharing he seeks, born of anger and revenge as well as of identification. He is not drawn to the element of beauty in Elvire's love for Colino; rather, he sees it as sordid. But the sordidness which Nicolo sees in Elvire's liaison with Colino and which links her private world with his own affair with Xaviera has a more complicated side to it. If Nicolo views his own relationship with Xaviera with some shame it is because it has been judged as despicable by his step-parents, and he has sought to hide the relationship because of that moral judgment. It is a judgment which affects not only his view of the relationship but also, and perhaps on a deeper and even more important level, his own self-conception and feelings of self-worth. His embarassment and dishonesty about Xaviera and about his relationship with her are attitudes which clearly were learned.

When Nicolo's suspicion that Elvire leads a double life is confirmed, it is confirmed in a way that for him raises startling and infuriating parallels to his own double life. Of the step-parents it was Elvire who disapproved most of his liaison with Xaviera from the beginning, disapproving in particular of his attraction to Xaviera at the "early" age of fifteen; and yet Elvire's love for Colino had begun when she herself was only thirteen. Also, Nicolo's relationship with Xaviera had begun some five years before his form marriage with Constanze during which he of course continued to see Xaviera.[5] Now he learns that Elvire had fallen in love with Colino at least two years prior to her marriage with Piachi, a marriage which also reveals itself to be a marriage in form only. Although their situations seem parallel and potentially capable of producing some feeling of solidarity in Nicolo, this is true only in a limited fashion. The parallels combine with Nicolo's mistaken belief that Elvire was behind his public humiliation at the hands of Piachi -- because Nicolo believes she had reported to Piachi the presence of Xaviera's maid in Nicolo's chambers -- and any feeling of solidarity is perverted. He does not transfer to Elvire's situation whatever good he feels to exist in his relationship with Xaviera.

It must also be noted, however, that he does not condemn her "relationship," either. His anger does not spring from any sort of moral disapprobation but rather from the fact that he believes he has suffered from moral condemnation by the woman who leads a double life so very similar to his own. That the gentle Elvire suffers more from her double life than she revels in it, and that it is possible that her disapproval of his attraction to women at an early age was meant in some sense to protect him are considerations which do not enter his thoughts here. He is blind to the former consideration, and the latter was never a subject for discussion in the house. Like so many of Kleist's characters, Nicolo reacts out of complex and contradictory emotions -- out of comprehension and hurt, out of identification and hatred. They share a secret that has elements of the sordid as well as of the beautiful. It is clear that he is bound to her in a way from which Piachi is excluded.

Piachi has no hope for even such a bizarre fulfillment as Nicolo attempts to achieve. Much as Piachi would like to be the loving husband of a doting wife, he is married to her in form only. Her heart belongs to Colino, and he must endure the recurring frustration of seeing his wife retire to her chambers to see her lover. He is the odd man out in every way; he has lost his first wife and his son, and his second wife and adopted son do not in any sense replace them. To support his life he has only the form of a marriage and of a family, not the substance. If one can speak of a hidden world in his case, it is only one of unexpressed longing, frustration and loneliness. He loses to Colino, and to Nicolo as well.

The premises of the "Findling" are similar to those in the "Marquise," but the setting is filled with different and weaker characters. The Graf must struggle with his public image but he can do so with much success, and he is finally capable of seeing that he can be happy only when integrated into the real environment. He strives to make his person and his public image coincide in actual success. Nicolo, on the other hand, is far weaker than the Graf; he retreats to a private life which in some respects is as shallow as the life of appearances he leads for his stepparents. Although it is only in the fact of a private life, away from the disapproving eyes of his step-parents, that he can assert himself, even in that hidden life he is not autonomous. Xaviera is kept by the Bishop and her relationship with Nicolo is hardly unencumbered. His "friends," the Carmelites, want his future wealth and use him, feigning friendship and approval of him as himself and of his actions. But he is really manipulated object in that case as well. Nonetheless, the illusion of freedom and independence is real to him, because at least he is free to do what he wants. Nicolo is as much victim throughout as manip- ulator. In some measure, he does not attempt to realize his desire to assert himself by achieving actual success; rather, he tries to assert himself by merely negating in private what he is compelled to be in public.[6] He is a son in form only; and in the costume of Colino he is a pathetic travesty of the cavalier, lacking all the qualities of strength and nobility which the cavalier had demonstrated when he saved Elvire.

Piachi is also weak, a failure as a father and, in his own eyes, as a husband unable to gain even the attention, much less the affection, of his wife. He simply avoids any attempt to compete with Colino. It is sad, and pathetic, too, to see him forsake any hope of salvation and instead seek till the end of time to avenge on an unworthy opponent the destruction of a marriage that never was, the loss of a house that was never a home and of great wealth that bought him nothing of value. He cannot even nourish a hope of being united with Elvire in death. Even a token union in death, as between Toni and Gustav, is missing. One must note that the nature of his vengeance betokens his rage at the loss of the shell of his marriage and the shell of his life, not primarily at the loss of Elvire. He seems to exist only in the forms in which he lives and in whatever fantasies he may have.

Elvire displays her charitable nature only in private; she reveals warmth neither to Piachi nor to Nicolo. Unlike the retreat of Julietta which she terminates out of love for her children and which causes her sadness, the retreat of Elvire is a withdrawal away from a reality she never gains the strength to cope with and into dreams of a past that never materialized. She lacks the strength of Julietta, who retains dignity in defeat and develops a nobility through her reemergence into the world. With the debasement of the content of her private world, Elvire withers and dies.

There is no desire to make the forms work in the "Findling" as there was in the "Marquise." In this counterexperiment, social frameworks and proper form are not erected to live by, but in order to cover what is not there. It is not so much a story of deception as one of manipulation of exterior appearances. Though it is a story of people erecting facades and existing through appearances, as we find in many of Kleist's works, in the extremity of the development they cease to be people. In this story, both the facades and the private worlds represent a lack of confrontation with what is real and a withdrawal into fictions.

It is difficult to separate the psychological issues from the existential issues in these cases. As much as one might understand the practical motivations for Gustav's or the Graf's manipulations and self-delusions, for example, it must still be admitted that their mental acrobatics soon give rise to problems of self-definition and to existential problems. It is in this aspect of retreat from the real world that Kleist examines the question of whether such retreats into private realities represent existence at all. The various threats which confront Kleist's characters can occasion extreme withdrawals.

In the extreme case of being confronted with annihilation, the response is quite obvious and comprehensible. In his initial reaction to his death sentence, for example, Prince Friedrich reacts by blurting out his willingness to renounce the world, loyalty, honor, esteem, society, love, and his past. His consciousness focuses on the smallest possible point: physical survival. And he really gives up everything, every context through which an individual can come to a self-definition; reduced to its smallest point his consciousness does not even include a sense of his own self. His desire to retreat to his estate on the Rhine strikes one not so much as a return to the simplicity of nature -- the recurring cycle of sowing and harvesting he initially describes. Rather, the cyclical quality he describes has a hollow and ultimately meaningless quality to it: "und in den Kreis herum das Leben jagen, bis es am Abend niedersinkt und stirbt"(1035-6).

But others of Kleist's characters react in a similar fashion of withdrawal even though they are not confronted directly with the certainty of physical annihilation. The threats to many of Kleist's characters need not be as concrete nor as certain as that. Some of these characters evade the contexts in which they live and attempt to retreat from any existence in the world at all.

Johann, in Schroffenstein, is an extreme example of this fear of living. He is not social and has no image in social contexts.

Unable to cope with the terrors that existence holds for him he feels only the weight of existence itself: "Es hat das Leben mich wie eine Schlange, mit Gliedern, zahnlos, ekelhaft, umwunden. Es schauert mich, es zu berühren"(1048-9). He utters this statement of despair in a sentence in which he appears only as the direct object, one notes, while life is the active subject. He withdraws so far from all contexts that one looks in vain for a real personality in him. He seems to need a stable and timeless realm in order to exist; he needs to be saved from life, redeemed from existence itself. He does not love Agnes; he needs Maria, a saving concept that has nothing to do with continued life or with another person.

It is not love in any case, which would imply a social context of at least two people. Maria does not exist in this world for him, and he attaches himself to the very lack of context which that signifies for him. He says to Maria, "Ach, lieben! Ich vergöttre dich!"(1033) The creation of the Maria phantom out of Agnes presents him, or so he believes, with that possibility of moving out of space and time, and he fixes his sights on the moment when she met him: "den Augenblick, wo segensreich, heilbringend, ein Gott ins Leben mich, ins ewge führte"(261-2). The life he refers to is not life at all, of course, and he eventually asks Maria-Agnes to destroy him physically; salvation and destruction are inextricably mixed for him. Johann stands outside the action, incapable of acting and unwilling to engage in reality at all; even his death must be at someone else's hands. His pastlessness in the play, as one who has never acted and thus never created a self in the world, is much like Sartre's Orestes in Les Mouches. Kleist's symbolic representation of this is that Johann is the bastard, the parentless one who does not belong to Rossitz, nor to Warwand, the other pole of reality in the play.

Johann is not the only character who is crushed by an awareness of the risk of living, but, along with Penthesilea he is the most extreme. Other heroes and heroines display a similar distaste for life and for the physicality of existence. Littegarde in the "Zweikampf" lives in retreat much as does the Marquise. The ethereal Käthchen, in what works as a comical scene, flees the garden terrified when she happens upon Kunigunde and is presented with the base physical realness of what Kunigunde is; Käthchen seems to feel a revulsion from anything physical.

Julietta is a figure who, until near the end of the story, lives largely in withdrawal. To complete the discussion of her, begun above in a different context, it can be observed that Julietta has been a withdrawn person at least from the time of her husband's death before the story begins. She had left the estate reluctantly after that and then lived within the bosom of the minimal social unit of her family, "in der größten Einge-zogenheit," we are told(104). She swears never to enter marriage again, and she uses a telling formula: "ich mag mein Glück nicht ... auf ein zweites Spiel setzen"(117). That she views any extension of her self into the flux of reality as a risk is made obvious by her actions thus far in the story. Her activities are conservative and retentive rather than open and assertive; she takes care of her parents and her children; she is the caretaker

of the borders of her world. What is implicit in her statement,
however, is that the risk is too great, that she will lose in any
confrontation with reality, that it represents a hazard to touch
another -- in particular, another man. Larger, fluid contexts of
society hold no draw for her at all.

Julietta's alienation from herself when she becomes certain
of her pregnancy is compounded in a dreadful fashion when she is
cast out from the house. She is stripped of her moral and social
status and is forced into a retreat that is even further from
social existence. She withdraws to the smallest possible social
unit, her children, and to her self. She does not find fulfillment in the corridors of the self but is, rather, reduced to a
static point outside the flux of reality. The pride with which
she arms herself against the incursions of the world becomes a
conscious obliteration of the outside world. Pride here is only a
sustaining attitude in a qualified manner, for at this point it is
a private virtue with no social existence.

In her withdrawal she resembles Johann now much more closely,
needing a stable and timeless realm in order to exist. The
withdrawal from space and time is suggested not only by the
physical situation but by formulations which contrast events which
occur in the world with the stasis and suspension of time in her
ordered retreat:

> Und so war der **Zeitpunkt**, da der Graf F... von Neapel
> wiederkehren sollte, noch nicht abgelaufen, als sie schon
> völlig mit dem Schicksal, in **ewig** klösterlicher Einge-
> zogenheit zu leben, vertraut war. (126, emphasis mine)

There is a tension in Kleist's works, between existence and attempted solipsism, between existing in the flux of the historical plane and the characters' attempts to make the world and others their own by altering their experience of the world and others, by altering what they themselves do and know, in the service of their fantasies and fears. But Kleist does not let his characters retreat to this ahistorical stasis. He drags them back to where he insists they find a way to exist: in the world.

Chapter 11

IDENTITY AND EXISTENCE

The existence of facades, and the existence of private worlds
which are not real -- at least in the sense that they do not enter
the historical plane -- present several problems which clearly
fascinate Kleist, for he repeatedly weaves these types of activity
around each other. The problem of how people can interact at all
under such circumstances is one of these problems, and the
discussion will turn to that shortly, but the central problem
associated with facades, private realities, and manipulation of
experience, is that of identity.

Kleist draws the reader's attention again and again to the
fact that his characters can be only what they are allowed to be
by others, regardless of what the characters themselves believe
they are or what they have talked themselves into believing they
are. In an environment where no one else will confirm their
knowledge of themselves, Littegarde and Julietta cannot maintain
themselves as who they think they are. The assault is on their
unity of experience, their identity, and it pushes both of them to
the rim of insanity. Julietta's defensive swoon and subsequent
flight to her walled-in estate have their counterpart in the
"Zweikampf" in Littegarde's swoon and later in a nearly autistic

withdrawal into herself in prison after Trota has ostensibly lost the duel and all the world and the heavens have proclaimed that she is someone she has no knowledge of: she lies on the straw, "wie eine Wahnsinnige, ohne zu hören und zu sehen"(250). And she states that as long as she is on earth she wishes to see no other person. The very gaze of Trota, who has, she feels, been the agent of the annihilation of her identity, she finds "entsetzlich, unerträglich, vernichtend!"(251) And each of these words may be taken literally.

In this regard and at this point both Julietta and Littegarde are in a very vulnerable and a very passive position. The basic tenet that Kleist continually draws attention to -- that one is what one has done, that one's identity is determined by one's acts -- has a perverse and paralyzing result here. Acts which do not belong to Littegarde and Julietta approach them and attach themselves to their persons, and they are caught, trapped, and defined. Each displays a kind of horrified fascination as things which do not emanate from their experience relentlessly float towards them and cling to them. In Julietta's case it is the apparent betrayal by her body as it slowly swells in indictment against her; in Littegarde's case it is her ring which, from her point of view, materializes where it could not possibly -- in Jakob's possession. Things which they recoil from as being alien to their person become evidence of a self they do not know. Things which they know to be not part of them become more substantial than their own selves.

Julietta's and Littegarde's predicaments are akin to Sylvester's, who is told he is a murderer in complete contradiction to his knowledge of self. In that case, of course, Sylvester capitulates and abandons his identity and accepts the label which has been attached to him, and he retains less and less of himself as the play progresses. In this he seems much like Rupert who, seeking Agnes in the mountains in order to kill her, has occasion to state, referring to Warwand's accusation against him, "Sie haben mich zu einem Mörder gebrandmarkt boshaft im voraus. --Wohlan, so sollen sie denn recht gehabt auch haben" (2248-50). In point of fact, however, it is important to recognize that Rupert is not at all as malleable as Sylvester, at least not in quite the same way. Much like a Jean Genet retaining his freedom behind a criminal role put on him by others, Rupert does not move into that role of murderer with any honesty, or so he believes. Rupert shifts a perception of himself to the outside, blaming Warwand for the murder he is about to commit. It is motivated by a refusal to accept his own guilt and accept the direction of his will. He restructures the state of affairs, displaces the event, and seemingly retains his innocence by accusing Warwand of making him a murderer by verbally defining him as one -- a reductive process he has used himself, of course. As a moral defense mechanism it works reasonably well for Rupert, who can actually commit a murder now and externalize the responsibility by shifting to Warwand the linguistic tampering with people and with reality. It is a playing with someone else's playing with words, a linguistic creation of a linguistic creation. Rupert's identity is damaged and eaten away at a deeper level, far below his conscious thoughts. It is only when, looking into a pool of water, Rupert is shocked and frightened to look into the eyes looking back at him, the eyes of a murderer, that we and Rupert realize that his moral sense of self has been seriously and genuinely undermined. Sylvester's sense of self collapses far more quickly under the fixing gaze of others, and he loses himself in the world.

Another recurring aspect of the power which others have over characters' sense of identity strikes those characters in particular who are endowed with a weak sense of self at the outset. There are several of these characters in Kleist's works, notably Käthchen and Kunigunde, Johann, and Penthesilea. They all have such an insubstantial and unstable awareness of identity that one is not amiss in referring to a vacuum of personality.

In many ways, Käthchen von Heilbronn is a schematic representation of several of the problems treated in this study. It is a play notably thin in psychological development of characters, and one notices quite easily the symmetrical arrangement of the figures. On the one side is Kunigunde, composed of lifeless elements of the earth, who has no place in the world save that which she manipulates men into granting her. On the other is Käthchen, silent and seemingly not of this earth, who also has no place in the world save that which is granted her by others. Strahl stands in the middle as the key figure for both Käthchen and Kunigunde.

Käthchen, before she is "activated" by Strahl's presence, is remarkably uninvolved with the world, and we know and learn nothing of the content of her personality. She has an odd but powerful sort of charisma that is marked by no emanation from her personality but rather by a complete lack of self-definition which causes others to project onto and into her their own feelings. When Strahl arrives on the scene, however, a remarkable change occurs. She becomes oriented entirely towards Strahl; as Blankenagel points out, "she lives, moves, and has her being in the man she loves."[1] She falls instantly under Strahl's power, even though he himself is unaware of that power, and she literally cannot live without him. If she is removed from his presence, her vital powers wane visibly, and Theobald, after forcing her to a cloister, allows her to return to Strahl lest she die.

Kunigunde, of course, is quite different from Käthchen in many respects. While Käthchen is a completely unreflective and unconscious non-being, Kunigunde is a completely reflective and conscious non-being. Kunigunde exists as surface and only as surface, her "essence" created at the make-up table.[2] In a variant from the Phöbus edition of the play, Kunigunde describes the construction of her identity:

Die Kunst, die du <Rosalie> an meinem Putztisch übst,
Ist mehr, als bloß ein sinnereizendes
Verbinden von Gestalten und von Farben.
Das unsichtbare Ding, das Seele heißt,
Möcht ich an allem gern erscheinen machen
Dem Totem selbst, das mir verbunden ist....
Ein Band, das niederhängt, der Schleif entrissen,
Ein Strauß, --was du nur irgend willst, ein Schmuck,
Ein Kleid, das aufgeschürzt ist, oder nicht,
Sind Züg an mir, die reden, die versammelt
Das Bild von einem innern Zustand geben. (901)

She is the manipulator of external appearances _par excellence_. Further, she can exist only in others' experience of her, in their confirmation of the appearances she supplies.

Strahl occupies such an important position between the two, because in the play both of them can exist only under his gaze; he brings them into being through the light of his consciousness. His name, "Strahl," is a functional identification of his role between the two women. He keeps both of them in suspense up until the last lines of the play. Because Kunigunde is not bound only to Strahl, her disappointment at Strahl's choice of brides is not as tragic as it would be for Käthchen. Kunigunde can seek out a new man to capture by means of her cultivated and manipulative facade.

A more realistic portrayal of this deep dependence of one person on another is in the character Johann. As was stated above, Johann is in a defensive position in relation to reality. He is not very dissimilar from Käthchen in that he has a peculiar spiritual quality that seems totally devoid of content. He feels constantly on the edge of extinction when confronted with reality, though, because he seems to sense the void within himself. He is afraid of others and of life itself because his fragile surface may collapse inward. The other half of this problem, of course, is represented by the feeling that he needs someone else to confirm that he exists at all. His creation, Maria, is the focus of this need which parallels Käthchen's dependence on Strahl. The ultimate paradox of Johann's predicament is seen in his approach to Agnes in the second act. After seeing that Ottokar is conquering the affections of Agnes, Johann fears that Maria simply "doesn't know that he is alive," a horrifying thought for someone as pathologically sensitive in his existence as Johann is.[3] When he approaches Agnes, he begs her to kill him: "Nimm diesen Dolch, Geliebte -- Denn mit Wollust, wie deinem Kusse sich die Lippe reicht, reich ich die Brust dem Stoß von deiner Hand"(1054-6). A paradox arises because of the combination of his fears concerning the threat of life on the one hand, and his desperate need for Maria's saving awareness of him on the other. He is at the extreme point where his destruction coincides with his salvation.

While it is not a surprise for modern man to be told that the individual comes into being through others and that the individual needs others to confirm his or her identity, the important position this theme occupies in Kleist's works has been largely overlooked in the critical literature. This complex of concerns draws further attention to itself not only because of the frequency with which it recurs in Kleist's works but also because of the extreme and pathological limits to which Kleist develops the question of what can be or might not be beneath the surface of people.

In a different context above, it was observed that Piachi lived in the forms of family roles without partaking of any of the essence of such roles. Although he is clearly not as insecure as someone like Johann, the extent to which Piachi truly exists -- is who and what he is -- in the roles he plays can be measured by the literally infinite rage which consumes him when he finds Nicolo has through a cheap sham taken even these roles -- and his house

and money, as well -- from him. Piachi's incommensurate vengeance, and the costs to Piachi of this vengeance, go beyond space
and time.

Finally, more akin to Johann's dreadful insecurity and fear
than is Piachi's or even Käthchen's, is Penthesilea's fragile
self. Her actions do not emanate from the level of will, for
which she would have to have the perspective to make decisions and
choices; rather, her actions are a pure reflection of her self's
defending its own structure. It is not a question of defending
the content of her self, for there is no fixed content to her
identity. Her inability to make clear decisions, the total
involvement with whatever activity she is engaged in at the moment
-- be it agressive or defensive -- the rapid and extreme
vacillation between love and hate for Achilles, between abject
fear of and total attraction to Achilles, the manner in which she
exists totally in fantasies or in the present without the solidity
which a firm past provides, all these things are caused by her
awful need to preserve her naked existence. It is impossible to
locate any essence in her at all; she is entirely defined by her
desperate defensive maneuvers aimed at preventing the loss of her
self which is only a surface covering a vacuum. Koch is quite
correct in observing that the tension in the play is not between
love and obligation to the Amazons, but rather, that her battles
are waged to find a place in the world where she can exist.[4]

The primary location of her battle is the space between her
and Achilles. On the one hand Achilles represents the ultimate
menace to her, threatening to extinguish her self by making it a

thing, an object to his subject. Though there is, of course, an element of that in Achilles' mind as well, he is not nearly as vulnerable as Penthesilea because he is quite capable of not engaging his entire being in the battle with her; as was discussed above, he already views her as an object which he controls from a superior position of freedom and play. On the other hand, Penthesilea is desperately attached to Achilles, who is the necessary confirmation of her existence. She shifts instantly and completely between these two extremes, consumed one moment with the monomaniacal need to destroy him, as she eventually does, symbolically and physically absorbing him into her, and consumed the next moment with the absolute and vital necessity to be absorbed by him, even, as was noted in the case of Johann, if such an encounter would coincide with her physical destruction.

Even when he is not there, she is capable of fabricating his presence in her own mind. At one point, for example, she is looking into the river and "sees" Achilles, really the reflection of the sun. Seconds before, she had spoken of destroying Achilles, -- she had been staring for several long minutes at the direct light of the sun which was beating down on her -- "Bei seinen goldnen Flammenhaaren zög ich zu mir hernieder <Helios>" (1384-5); now, she looks down into the river and turns instantly to the opposite extreme of needing Achilles to the point of her own physical destruction, and she moves to sink into the water: "Da liegt er mir zu Füßen ja! Nimm mich--"(1387). It is clearly not love which we witness in such scenes; there is no possibility of their existing together. Penthesilea is in the awful situation, due to the pathological insecurity which marks her experience of her self, of being unable to exist in his presence as well as of being unable to exist away from his presence.[5]

Kleist's characters are obviously not all as fragile and threatened by others as Penthesilea is; rather, Kleist creates in his works an entire scale of responses by individuals to the presence of others. Characters such as Hermann and Achilles have, or think they have, security and freedom in the realm of play, and they toy with others. Penthesilea and Johann, and Käthchen and Kunigunde in a schematic way, are at the other end of the scale, vulnerable, absolutely and vitally, to the presence and manipulations by others. In between, as we have seen, there is a free-for-all in the wide range of experiments Kleist conducts in which characters jockey for control of situations and environments. While the degree of damage which may occur to the self varies greatly from character to character depending on the constitution of the individual, it is apparent that the outcome of the games for control are of import for self-definition in nearly every case. The games discussed throughout this study represent battles for space in which to exist, whether only in private worlds or in the fray of interaction.

The problems discussed in this chapter do not represent insoluble conundrums for either Kleist or his characters, however. Locating and defining a place to exist in contexts with other people is no easy task for Kleist's characters, and some of them have no chance for survival because the delicately poised way in which they are constituted makes a secure existence impossible. But a few characters can establish and gain perspective on themselves and their place in the world, even if the perspective and knowledge they gain may not always be welcome. Many of the ways Kleist's characters set out to create who and where they are are mendacious and inauthentic in nature. Characters' manipulation of their own experience and of others' experience, the retreats to fantasies and to private realities, the games played with the world and with others, do not, on the whole, represent a genuine encounter with the world, with others, or with themselves. Many of the characters deny where, when, and who they are.

Kleist, however, does force several of his characters to confront the contexts in which they exist, driving them from their illusions and retreats, shattering the games they play. For despite the pervasiveness of the characters' inauthentic way of dealing with themselves, others, and the world, this mechanism is not the message in Kleist's works; what his characters do is not necessarily what Kleist is doing in his works. In fact, Kleist continually destroys the existential and moral validity of such dynamics and robs his characters of success in their manipulations and self-delusions. Kleist frequently builds an irony into the stories he creates, causing to fail precisely those characters who try most ambitiously to control the world about them. Kunigunde fails in her attempts as do Congo Hoango, Piachi, Adam, and Achilles, for example.[6] And in the nexus of their stories Rupert, Penthesilea, Amphitryon, and the Graf are characters whose determination to preserve themselves and to alter or deny what goes on about them ironically leads to the threat of greater disaster. In Kleist's view the attempt to control what is, a grasping and at times solipsistic attempt to own the world, is not likely to be a path to living a life well.

Though Kleist's works resist reduction to any single message, it is appropriate now to take note of the same problem from another perspective which offers in a limited fashion a solution to some of the problems his characters face. Kleist's works are also about the process of characters' confronting or being forced to confront the demands and power of the world outside themselves and through that to confront what they themselves are. Frequently painful, it is very much a process of -- literally -- realization, realization of the self in its inescapable contexts of other people. The question of identity and self-definition is a marked presence in all of Kleist's works. Now, characters certainly probe into the identity of others, asking "who are you?" or perhaps "who are you really?" This is the questioning of Babekan and Toni when they meet Gustav and of his questioning of them. It is Achilles' asking Penthesilea what he should call her and Strahl's confronting the mystery that is Käthchen: "O du - - - wie nenn ich dich? Käthchen! Warum kann ich dich nicht mein nennen? Käthchen, Mädchen, Käthchen!"(685-7) It lies behind the probing questioning by the Marquise's mother at Julietta's estate and by Ruprecht when he confronts Eve. But, as has been shown, the issue of who other people are becomes quickly enmeshed with the question of self-definition. For Amphitryon it is not so much a question of who Jupiter is, after all, but one of the reality of his own self and the validity of his own experience; the latter becomes the issue for Alkmene as well when she realizes that she can no longer trust her own knowledge of who her husband is and when she must doubt the validity of her memory and experience.

The problem that resides near the thematic center of these stories and which joins the problems of facades and private worlds and manipulations is the problem of identity and of location of the self in the world. This is true not just for characters such as Amphitryon who are completely displaced, both physically and in the minds of all who know him. The question of who and how characters are to be is also apparent in more subtle ways. Agnes, whi is coming of age, has, both in fact and symbolically, not yet been baptized at the beginning of Schroffenstein, and who she is and will become and how she will relate to others in any sort of a secure existence are not only a problem for her, as we see in the extreme to which she goes to relate to Ottokar; her christening as Maria is of similar import to Ottokar's and especially Johann's way of thinking about themselves.

Likewise, Toni is re-christened in the "Verlobung" and it is instrumental to the radical change in the way she thinks about who she is and how she will relate to others; and, as shown above, the renaming of Toni alters Gustav's sense of his place in the world as well. As another example, in the nasty circumstances into which they are thrust and because of the way they are forced unwillingly into roles by others, Gustav and Nicolo have trouble finding a way to feel at all good about their lot or themselves; their need to feel regarded as worthy human beings is in danger of

being thwarted. Gustav finds himself shown to the very room where
the plantation owner was infected as he was fleeing, and Nicolo
finds himself in the room, clothes, and life of Paolo. The
incident in the "Findling" with the six small ivory letters, while
certainly of enormous importance for the progress of the plot when
Nicolo fortuitously forms the name "Colino" from them and Elvire
notes it, has a more pathetic side to its history. The letters
are not only the sole remaining toys from Nicolo's youth; they
were clearly the most important "toys" he had. The image evoked,
that of the child Nicolo's "playing" with the six small letters,
his arranging of and watching the fragments that form his name,
suggests a sad anchor for his sense of self in that environment
where he has never been allowed to be or develop his self.

In all of these cases and in others it is apparent that the
characters cannot live alone in the world. Though they may not
live in any true relatedness to other individuals, especially at
the outset of their stories, they cannot live independently of the
influence of others either. In the last analysis, Kleist's
characters are not allowed to be solipsistic. Problems arise not
because characters truly live in isolation from other people but
because the fortunes and predicaments of the characters become
inextricably bound up with those of others.

In "Die Marquise von O..." the Graf's predicament and the
Marquise's have a remarkable affinity and underlying unity, not
only because their predicaments stem from the same incident but
also because their subsequent existential crises are so similar.
The story is structurally and emotionally an intricate, delicate

ballet with the two characters changing and developing in separate yet linked inner movements. As in many of Kleist's works, a deed seeks to attach itself to someone who does not at all want it. This is true of the "assignations" in the Krug and in the "Zweikampf," of the "sin" in the "Erdbeben," of the "disobedience" of Homburg, of the "murders" of the herald and the child in Schroffenstein. Something, an event which is uncaused, which in a sense "just happened," becomes a dreadful determinant of someone's identity and existence. In the "Marquise," we wonder less about how the Graf could have done such a thing than about how he can survive the consequences -- and how Julietta can survive them. For him if not for us, however, the problem is more complex. He must come to terms with that seemingly impossible, certainly inexplicable, deed, as must Julietta. The Graf and Julietta move through a long process in doing so, one that changes them both in substantial ways.

The initial impact of the illicit encounter on the Graf and Julietta is one of alienation from their own selves. The Graf must ask himself how he, an honorable and decent man, could have committed such a crime; Julietta must ask how such a crime could be hers. This alienation, which in the end proves to be a necessary step and a positive development in the process of coming to an understanding of what it means to exist, is hardly welcomed by either of them. The way out of their plight is not made easy for either of them by Kleist.

The Graf's initial remorseful attempt at atonement through quick death in battle does not succeed, and his problem is compounded and intensified when he is praised for his valor. His attempts to avoid accepting responsibility for the act, based in part on his unwillingness to acknowledge to his inner self that he has done what he has done and his understandable unwillingness to be the person who committed the crime and in part on the clear recognition of the practical consequences which would be sure to follow, are also not allowed to succeed, neither as the self-delusion of believing he and Julietta could avoid shame and misfortune simply through the legitimizing institution of marriage nor as the self-delusion of the phantom idyllic retreat in which he suggests he and Julietta might exist. Rather, he is forced into a moral confrontation with himself and with the issues of moral and existential responsibility. The difficulty of resolving these dilemmas is more acute for him than for Julietta because she at least "knows" that she is not responsible for her predicament. And as he comes to love her as a person and no longer sees her merely as the agonizing evidence of his crime, the stress on him becomes unbearable. He must somehow reveal himself to save both Julietta and his conscience or he will be destroyed; yet in saving Julietta and himself he will be destroyed. He has reached an impasse.

Now, exactly like the Graf, Julietta is horrified to learn that everything she knows of herself, her knowledge of her character, and the unity of self which is based on what she knows of her past actions -- her identity -- has been destructively undermined. Like the Graf she has and yet has not done something impossible and is alienated from herself utterly. Her initial denials also fail for obvious reasons and she is forced into a retreat to save the self that has become illusory. But the walled-in retreat of Julietta's estate is not where the practical or existential solution can be found for either the Graf or Julietta. Julietta reflects painfully on the same issues of moral responsibility that plague the Graf. The difficult yet central aspect of jurisprudence, self-sameness -- that to judge a person responsible for an act that person must be the same person who committed the act -- is resolved here in what is really an astonishing fashion. Julietta accepts the deed which has attached itself to her even though she cannot find the self which did it.

The problem is not primarily a practical one but one of how she chooses to exist. Her decision is one made through careful deliberation and is clearly courageous, for the announcement in the newspaper is if anything even more scandalous than her pregnancy itself. In her acceptance, she gives up the hold on herself which could be preserved only in her retreat and gains a very new sense of what she is. She literally incorporates the deed into herself, and she opens herself to the world at the same time in a mutual infusion of self and world. She becomes aware of her physical existence, something which many of Kleist's characters are prone to deny. The Marquise learns not only that her body knows things that she does not, but also that she _is_ her body. Her re-emergence into the real world coincides with her acceptance of that fact. She also comes to accept the fact that who she is is dependent on others' experience of her: whether or not the pregnancy is a result of her own will, the deed becomes part of her historical self -- that is where she must live. Her public announcement in the newspaper is the turning point of the novella. The structure of the novella underscores the importance of the decision. Everything that is artificial in the story -- her various retreats, her denials, the Graf's manipulative games and self-delusions -- is enclosed between the opening lines of the novella which relate the newspaper announcement, and the point in the chronological sequence of events where she decides to place the announcement in the newspaper.

Her decision and bid to reenter the world and her recognition of what it means to exist -- in the world and for others -- precipitates a similar reflex in the Graf. Her announcement in the newspaper opens the way for him out of his impasse and for him also finally to accept responsibility for the deed, both publicly and to himself. He responds to her in the newspaper also, and in so doing feels a relief from his secret burden, relaxes in the knowledge that he will reveal himself, not only to the Marquise, but to the world. He makes his decision while standing at the window looking outward to the world, not into himself. He also uses the newspaper, that public organ of communication, rather than a letter to the Marquise. This last maneuver is not theatrics on his part. In the announcement is revealed an intelligent understanding of the situation and a sensitivity for Julietta's distress and her desires. He selects her parents' house as the venue of revelation. It is not merely because he wishes to complete the painful process of confession to all concerned at one time; given the determined tone of his "jetzt weiß ich, was ich zu tun habe," the move is also designed to effect the reconciliation of Julietta with her parents.

The interval between the appearance of his announcement and the appointed hour is, we can calculate, at least seven days, which allows sufficient time for the reconciliation to take place. Aside from the relative patience the Graf demonstrates here in contrast to his consistently urgent pushing earlier, we also sense the gradual yet very significant reassertion of specific time and explicit intervals into the narrative. And with that event -- on the third, at the Commandant's house, at 11:00 precisely -- the Marquise and the Graf reenter the flux of reality, released from the suspension that marked their lives of secrets and of private worlds.

After a familial discussion of the proper form of reception, mother and daughter sit in formal dress awaiting the visitor in a tableau of ritual-like expectation. The Graf makes an entrance rather than one of his mysterious appearances, and his arrival as part of a gradual process helps to restore a sense of reality and real time to his relationships with others. Entering in the exact uniform he wore on that infamous night, he brings the family, and the reader, full circle back to the beginning. It marks a return to that moment when the break in the lives of Julietta and the Graf occurred. After some time and after they are married for a second time, they are clearly very different people, however, than they were at the outset -- open to each other and to the world in a way which they were previously not, aware that they are not an absolute self but rather existent, incarnate, and responsible.

Julietta's taking of the Graf's act upon herself saves the
Graf; it is what forces and allows him to complete the process of
self-realization.   It is one of the ironies of the story that he,
who has been the manipulator in the story and who cannot find a
way to save himself or Julietta, is saved by the person who was
the victim, that he who attempts to dictate the scenario of what
will happen must follow the lead of Julietta.[7]   It is also ironic
that the Graf's violation of Julietta which causes such alienation
from her self is the incident that will ultimately bring her to
her self.   In Kleist's choreography of the story it is the Graf's
violation of Julietta and his pressure on her through the story
which ironically serve the positive function of forcing her out of
the withdrawn existence which she had chosen to lead; she who
dared not place herself at risk ends up courageously risking
everything, and winning.

To win, of course, she sacrifices the sure hold which she had
maintained on her self.   It is this willingness to open herself
this way and realize herself in the contexts of the world and
others which breaks the deadlock in the cycle of manipulation,
mistrust, and illusion which had marked so many aspects of
relationships in the story.   It is parallel to the carefully
conscious decision of Agnes in Schroffenstein to risk her very
life in an attempt to relate to Ottokar; the other possibility, of
not risking, becomes to her at that moment too stifling a way of
living.

The realization of Julietta and the Graf that they are their
bodies and that they are what they have done is a sort of

perspective which, though it seldom occurs in Kleist's works,
represents a model of sorts for authentic existence. For other
characters, though, these confrontations with the only real
contexts of existence leave no mark. Käthchen is certainly
reminded of her corporeality when in ethereal longing she walks
out the window of her father's peculiarly located blacksmith shop
in pursuit of Strahl, and promptly plummets thirty feet to the
pavement and breaks both legs, just above the kneecap. Kleist
clearly is not so much expecting the withdrawn Käthchen to come to
any significant realization out of the incident, but he does point
out the absurdity of her non-physical sense of self. In his
works, Kleist seems more interested in the variations on the
mechanism of the problem than he is in prescribing a cure and
solution that would not work for many of his all too credible
characters, who in their weaknesses and illusions dare not risk
opening themselves to others and to the world. Most of them
remain unaware of -- or deny -- the subjectivity of others and
attempt to remain free by controlling the world through the
manipulation of experience.

Some others, however, do come to a similar awareness of
themselves and of their relationship to others and to the world
even if the results within the stories are not as felicitous as
that of the "Marquise." Prince Friedrich reaches his moral high
point when he accepts the fact that he is responsible for his
earlier precipitous act of disobedience even though the act was
not an issue of his conscious will. He, too, comes to realize
that he is what he has done, that he must be the legend which his

actions have created.[8]   Homburg's recognition of his responsibility to himself and to others is bought at an extreme price, of course: his acceptance of the death penalty at the moment when he realizes what it means to live one's life well.[9]   The outcome which Homburg consciously anticipates here does not happen, and perhaps there is an unfortunate cruelty, from a moral and existential point of view at any rate, in the way the Elector yanks him away from this moment of feeling fulfilled back into "life" with a recapitulation of the dream sequence from the first scene of the play.

That self which Homburg had come to view as less authentic because of its unearned, illusory, and unattached nature is suddenly lauded as worthy and more real and more "his" than his own new sense of self; he must now ask if he is in a dream, and his sense of reality and of identity is yet again undermined. Given the moral elegance with which the Prince stands before us at the end of the play, however, and given his success in withstanding his alienation from himself and, indeed, his coming to himself through it, it is certain he will survive this disorientation. While the Elector's toying with Homburg in this scene adds little to Homburg's sense of self, one should note that the Elector's toying with Homburg in the first scene and his sentencing of Homburg to death later unintentionally serve a positive function: the resulting alienation of Homburg from himself is precisely what leads to his moral development.

In the "Verlobung" characters come to a new consciousness of themselves and to insight into what they are and can be, but once again Kleist sets up circumstances which do not result in an outcome as exemplary as that of the "Marquise." The case of Toni, as was shown above, is relatively clear. She realizes that the lie she has been living represents a prostitution of herself rather than any ethical or authentic existence. When presented with the model of Mariane by Gustav and when she reflects on the significance of choosing how to live, she makes her decision about who she is to be. Her breakthrough, the most significant one she can make, is not in the love she has for Gustav -- since the love has so many illusory aspects from both Toni's and Gustav's side -- but rather in the new moral perspective she gains on who she is and can be, a perspective she gains through reflection on the life and death of Mariane and through surveying her past life and actions, as did the Graf, Julietta, and Homburg.

In a particular sense she shares a similarity with Congo Hoango here, at least insofar as his past is reported by the narrator. The theme of individuals' being robbed of their own identity by being taught a role and being expected to fill a role is repeated in Hoango's past. The narrator, who has the point of view of a white, finds the change from slave to revolutionary in Congo Hoango strange and inexplicable. Congo -- "der in seiner Jugend von treuer und rechtschaffener Gemütsart schien" -- once saved the life of his owner and was, we are told, "von seinem Herrn ... mit unendlichen Wohltaten überhäuft worden" (160). But all of the "proofs of gratitude," which include a grant of emancipation, the opportunity to live in the plantation house, the position of overseer, the woman Babekan, and, as the crowning kindness, retirement at 60 and an inheritance, prove no protection for Congo's master. With the revolution Congo Hoango is one of the first to reach for the gun, and he kills his master.

What parallels Toni's change here and what Kleist suggests is that Congo Hoango's change is not from facade to revelation of his true and treacherously evil nature, from the _appearance_ of faithful servant to revolutionary. Rather, the very "kindnesses" which his master grants him serve to raise and broaden his perspective, once again through the process of alienation and reflection: partaking of the roles of both black and white, overseer and slave, without, however, belonging to either his people or to the French, he gains a freedom of vision from which he chooses a course of action and a firm self-definition. He joins the war, "bei dem er sich ganz verjüngte," we are told(161). This reference to his youth recalls that earlier mention of him as a youth when he had saved his master. He comes full circle, beginning again in a very different life with a very different self-definition, a negation of his former life, a life with the poles changed. It is, however, a vision and a self-definition that are corrupted by hatred, and it is ironic that the nature of his self-definition is what finally brings about the rebellion of Toni when she is abused in much the same way he had been.

Gustav's coming to an awareness of what he is is even less happy, though certainly thorough in the end. However threatened he actually is in this environment, throughout the story he never reaches out in a fashion which is honest, even to himself. He is called "the stranger" throughout the story, and he is indeed a stranger both to himself and to others, not so much because he is alienated from himself and others as because he is simply out of touch, absorbed with defending himself. The self-awareness to which he comes does not result from a process of reflection and moral choice, as in the examples discussed above; his perspective on who and what he is comes in a sudden flash of understanding when Strömli explains the error Gustav has made. He is confronted with himself as a killer. He first had lost the illusion of the idyll he had built with Toni when he thought Toni had betrayed him, and he now realizes he was the one who destroyed the possibility of the realization of that idyll when he killed her. As Toni dies he grasps her, physically, and metaphorically -- as the universe which had become and is the limits of his existence, of his past, present, and future. As she fades from life so does he. His existence had become inextricably bound up with Toni's, or perhaps Mariane-Toni's, a private world that now races towards nothing.

As she dies he is standing at the window, which previously was closed, a real and metaphorical barrier between him and all the contexts of reality. He surveys the world at dawn and knows himself, standing as judge over his life in all its past roles and actions, unable to deny his guilt in the deaths of the two women who loved him. The responsibility he accepts for his acts has none of the aura of purifying re-integration that the choices of Julietta, the Graf, and Homburg had, however. Unlike the situations of those characters and of Toni, there is simply nothing left to attach himself to, nothing to which he can hold, nothing remaining through which he can participate in the formation of the project which is life. Gustav in a sense reaches the position of moral arbiter of his future acts, a perspective which he shares with the above characters; he simply sees no future for himself in which he might act, for he has just destroyed it.

Gustav's position in the story is central. His voiced reveries to Toni and his manipulation of Toni in their initial encounters were partly intentional, of course, in his attempt to create and ensure safety for himself, but the effect is unwittingly of a much more significant nature for Toni than he can know. His reveries and manipulation result in the creation of her new identity, a person of moral beauty that transcends her former self. In the dynamics of the novella he performs the remarkable function of both bringing her into being and destroying her.

While one might make a similar claim for the Elector's effect on Homburg, the situations are not so parallel in respect to their effect on Gustav and the Elector. The vulnerability of Gustav lies behind all he does, and, ironically, he becomes his own victim. The Elector's own sense of self and his safety do not at all stand under the same hazards as do Gustav's. In this regard Gustav's fate is much more like Rupert's in Schroffenstein who in the attempt to save himself, and his people, destroys the thing he loves most -- his son, and with him the hope for the continuation of the house of Rossitz. In these cases it is not simply the defensiveness of the self that brings on the disaster, but rather

Kleist sets up situations where the energy put into lashing out at others is reflected back in full force.

Much the same can be said of the machinations and violently defensive maneuverings of Piachi and Nicolo and of the defense of the self that Penthesilea undertakes. In striking out at others they really end up destroying themselves. In the "Findling" and in Penthesilea, of course, Kleist sets up impossible situations for the characters, whose fates seem to stand under some awful necessity. These characters have a weakness that defeats them, a weakness not only and not primarily in their situations, but rather in the way they are constituted as personalities. The endings of these works are empty because the characters are crushed; nothing lies underneath their surface which can support a real self. Unlike the fruitful movement towards a new and clearer definition of the self which was noted in many of the characters discussed above, the motion in these works is an inexorable march to destruction. There are no children born in the marriage of Piachi and Elvire, and Nicolo's wife, Constanze, dies with her child in childbirth, symbolic manifestations of the sterility of relationships without hope and without a future.

There is a naked animal-like energy, a vital energy without humanity, with which Penthesilea destroys Achilles, and through that her own possibility of survival. A similar energy characterizes the final confrontation between Nicolo and Piachi, a confrontation which comes about when there no longer is any need for nor possibility of carrying on the games of manipulation and surface which perversely and painfully held them together for years; the sustaining if hollow roles they have played break down because their masks are torn away by the other, not because they choose to exist without them. In a very perverse sense, of course, Nicolo might be described as breaking out of the facade he has been living for Piachi and Elvire, though it is unintended on his part: he has legal control of the house at that point, and he exercises his legal position to banish Piachi from the house. Standing over Elvire and sending Piachi away, Nicolo is, as a final irony, even now not so much his own man as a usurper of the empty role that had been Piachi's.

Kleist sets up various models in his works which defy abstraction to a single pattern. It is ultimately inexplicable where the resources of personality come from in the characters portrayed in Kleist's works -- why, for example, Littegarde lacks the inner strength of Julietta. They are in very similar circumstances, accused, marked and defined by a crime which is not theirs. Littegarde is at long last saved by her champion, Trota, but her reaction to her predicament is basically one of defeat. Julietta, on the other hand, becomes her own champion and saves herself, and incidentally the Graf as well. Likewise, the Graf and Homburg are able to gain a unity of self on a high level after bringing their moral consciousness to bear on the fragments of their selves, while Sylvester capitulates, ceases to believe in his moral autonomy, and loses his identity.

Certainly some patterns in Kleist's works are demonstrated -- that the world does not belong to an individual. Those who delude themselves and live in illusions are likely to have the possibility of realization of those illusions destroyed. Similarly, it is shown that the world does not, as a rule, belong to manipulators. Achilles miscalculates terribly when he does not regard the needs of Penthesilea, and he pays an equally terrible price. The Graf's manipulations are not successful in the way he intends. Congo Hoango's manipulations of Toni and white colonials bring on the opposite of what was planned: his belief that Toni was his creation and tool proves false as she uses the same tricks to fool him as he had trained her to use on fleeing whites; Strömli's band catches Congo Hoango sleeping, lulled into the same sense of security he had used to catch earlier refugees. Gustav's similar belief that Toni is his turns out to be truer and yet less true than he can know. These attempts to control backfire in most instances.

Those willing to give up and capable of giving up their illusions and confront the real and living contexts in which they exist, contexts composed of other living subjects with their own demands, are rewarded not only with the gift of a greater humanity in their souls but also concretely. Homburg's dream in the end becomes real, though not in an unproblematic way as we have seen, when he opens himself to the responsibilities he has. The Graf, after relinquishing his delusions and his dishonest approach to Julietta, is rewarded in the end with the marriage and the retention of his honor, the very things which he stood to lose through revealing himself. And in the end Julietta is enhanced in her moral essence and reputation far more than she had been before -- purer than the angels, as her mother says. Characters who gain sufficient perspective to realize that there is a minimal moral "ought" involved in existing and that it means realizing that one has to exist in the light of others' consciousness also receive another reward: these characters lose that great fear of releasing hold on their private worlds and themselves.

Chapter 12

PRIVATE WORLDS AND PUBLIC ROLES

Using the term "reality" in Kleist's works obviously can present
some problems since reality in these works seems frequently to
take on a very unreal quality. Kleist does not so much portray
the world in a given work as he presents us with a universe of
characters who bring their own worlds with them. The world of
things is of less importance to the dynamics of his works than the
way in which his characters experience that world. However,
Kleist's fascination with the workings of human subjectivity does
not result in a simple dichotomy between the self and reality.

In the complex of relationships that Kleist establishes in
his works, the idea of an unchangeable core of reality to which
man can refer does not come into question. This does not mean
that Kleist denies a reality outside the self, though.[1] While
Kleist's theoretical point of departure, as seen in his early
letters, may be the epistemological issue of the impossibility for
man of gaining unmediated knowledge of this core of reality, in
his works he develops a more refined view of the problem as he
takes note of the psychological makeup of individuals who are
placed into a world which is real but which has no inherent values
or meanings to provide support. Reality becomes relative because

it gains meaning only in relation to the experience of a given character. His characters are given the capacity to form meanings, and what is real becomes the projection of individual attitudes. His characters are not endowed with the capacity, however, as are Schiller's, to gain admission to a transcendental moral realm in which they can find stable support. Their freedom and their problems are greater than that: just as there is no unchangeable core of reality in Kleist's worlds, there is no unchangeable core to the self, and the self can define itself only in relation to the contexts in which it stands.

What results in the works is not unambiguously a joyous celebration of the liberation of man in existential and moral autonomy. Rather, his very human characters are, as Sartre said of modern man, condemned to freedom. The question then becomes not one of whether there are any real worlds but one of how individuals can create a space in which to exist in the one which they all must inhabit.

Kleist's characters, at least at the outset of works, do not engage in life as a project to be shared. They remind one of bubbles which float, isolated, through space, occasionally bumping into one another and registering some surprise and disorientation as they take note of the existence of others and some mistrust as they ask themselves whether they must make room for them. The notion that one can become part of a "we" is not the first impulse of Kleist's characters, and it is as rare as it is touching to hear a character willingly and effortlessly offer to share a life, as does Prothoe, for example:

Liegst du an meinem treuen Busen nicht?
Welch ein Geschick auch über dich verhängt sei,
Wir tragen es, wir beide: fasse dich. (1583-5)

While on a conscious level the characters may feel reasonably secure in their world -- in the ordering of their garden as it is metaphorically depicted in Sylvester's case -- the stability of the world of the individual characters is easily shaken and threatened by outside events and by the presence of others who intrude with demands from their own world. Rather than admit the world of their own experience is by nature a fiction, a private world, in the face of threats they are likely to alter what they are experiencing and create fictions in their environment, for themselves and for others, substituting a distorted reality for what they encounter outside themselves. And rather than admit that what they are, socially and existentially, is by nature a legend which comes into being through others as well as themselves, they are likely to try to preserve the shell of the legend that is their own view of themselves. To be prepared to change, to grow with the flux of new realities, as Prothoe exhorts Penthesilea to do in the above passage, is not an attractive proposition but rather a risk. To accept that others are the mirror in which we see ourselves represents a hazard rather than a support.

In the "Marionettentheater" essay Kleist suggests that the quality which separates man from immediacy with his environment and links him, in a very limited fashion, with God is the curse of reflection. In his works, though, the quality which separates man from nature and which distinguishes man from God, who simply "is," seems more precisely to be imagination -- the creative act of the mind, the capacity to envision what is not seen and to be conscious of things by means other than perception. This power of the mind to order and form is used to different ends by Kleist's characters and with very different results. The activity most frequently noted in this study was the creation -- and preservation -- of a self-structured reality that is actually an illusion. It represents more a refusal to see than an inability to see. An essential quality of the maintenance of illusion and the preservation of order is stasis, as can be seen, for example, in the frozen forms of existence in the "Findling," in the frozen self-delusions of Rupert who commits murders in the name of the preservation of morality while denying his own responsibility for immoral acts, in the resistance of Guiskard to allowing the mention of the word disease, or in the fantastic realms in which Gustav seeks to find refuge.

It is the inflexibility and closed quality of these illusions which in Kleist's works finally brings about their own destruction. It is not the fragility of the world which in the end defeats such characters, but rather the fragility of their ordering of the world.[2] The illusions and self-delusions of these characters are characterized by the attempt to create a space that is outside the most basic contexts, those of space, time, and the reality of co-existing in space and time with others. In Gustav's case, for example, his lack of touch with what is around him is not so much the result of his just not taking note of the present as it is of his attempt to exist out of time by existing in a different part of time, either in dreams of the future or in recall of the past. Gustav, much like the manipulative aesthetic seducer in Kierkegaard's "Seducer's Diary," avoids involvement in existence and in actual relationships, seducing others and himself into believing his own created images. This is also true of the phantom relationships of Elvire and Johann. The ideal -- of a Mariane, a Colino, or a Maria -- is not in itself a problem, and the adored figures are indeed the very model of positive and unselfish interaction with other people. But in imposing an order which does not fit, in substituting the unreal for the real, they miss the human essence of the other person; and by orienting their own existence to the phantom they also miss, indeed try to miss, the concrete environment in which they really are. Colino, Mariane, and Maria are figures from the past or the future which represent stability outside of time. These characters who seek freedom, ironically, become prisoners of their own subjectivity.[3]

The nature of the imaginative consciousness here differs from the nature of imagination for mainstream Romantics and is far more akin to a modern sense of consciousness. It is unlike the power of imagination as we find it in Schlegel or Novalis, in Blake, in Wordsworth or Coleridge, where the exercise of imaginative consciousness expands the soul and supples the means to gain access to higher truths and the infinite. Kleist presents here a conception of the imagination as an impoverished power which can limit knowledge and the soul. Because Kleist denies the possibility of escaping the world which man inhabits, imagination does not provide a way to transcend reality but merely serves to mask it. The imagination is, especially for its most active users, not an integrative faculty which seeks connections between phenomena or between the self and the world. Rather, it can divorce individuals from the world even as they attempt to make it their world.

The ideals in whose presence these characters try to exist do not result in the characters' salvation despite the image of savior that each of these figures represents. Johann, of course, fails in his attempt to have Agnes save him -- or destroy him, and with the failure he becomes insane instead. The phantoms of Colino and Mariane, also beautiful images of saviors, become instrumental in the ultimate destruction of the characters who cling to them: Elvire discovers Colino to be a shell, worse, a shell which has become inhabited by the antithesis of Colino; Gustav finds, so he believes, the terrible perversion of his ideal in the betrayal by Toni. Their lives are destroyed in that realization. Part of the reason this occurs is that the phantoms are attempted refuges from the necessity to confront reality directly.

These characters prefer to be saved rather than to acknowledge their capacity to make the decision to save themselves.[4] In this there also lies an element of bad faith; these characters, and Eustache for a similar reason, abdicate their moral responsibility to take control of the creation of what they are, avoiding making conscious decisions which would make them moral agents. In the examples given above there is not really a question of volition involved in the way they arrange their lives; like much that happens in and through Kleist's characters the actions originate on the level of the formation of the structure of consciousness, not on the conscious level of making decisions.

Also, in the examples given above, the creative act is one directed not really to life at all nor to creating a self in the contexts of life and of other people; their use of imagination reminds one once again of Sartre's critique of imagination. The phantoms are, or become, so attractive to Johann, Elvire, and Gustav in part precisely because they are not real and are not real people with demands of their own. They cling to the images they create out of the sense that while people and things may deceive them, their images of those people and things will not. To them, although not to the reader, it is reality which deceives. Finally, in the exercise of the imagination, the moral sensibilities of the characters can atrophy because the characters replace the humanity of others with a subjective and unchanging image.

The creative act need not, and in the patterns developed in Kleist's works indeed ought not, be directed toward living in the inner world. That use of the imagination does not represent a possibility for transcendence of reality. Kleist in his works gives several examples of characters who move out of a state of stasis in which so many other characters remain, and into the flux of the world, into an awareness of life as a process and as a project, a life for which they are both the creator and the creation, a life for which they are morally responsible, to others as well as to themselves. The nature of the sense of self which these characters develop is not an absolute sense of self, however, but a relative one: relative because it is based on a new-found awareness of their changing relationship to themselves and on their fluid dependence on the way others around them experience them.

Kleist's characters who develop this sense of self arrive there through a painful sort of birth as the stable world of their experience is torn from their grasp. We noted this process with several characters, each of whom is fragmented into more than one self, becoming a stranger to self and world. In essence, they are forced to confront an alter-ego and through that discovery they come to themselves. There are two "Grafen," two Juliettas, two Tonis, two Homburgs -- one known to others but not known to themselves, the other a sense of self that is not known to others.[5] They first experience that they are not who they think they are.

It is not a coincidence that these characters are victims of others' manipulations or abuse.[6] Having been treated as an object by others, they encounter themselves for the first time, seeing themselves in part as a thing yet at the same time becoming aware of the eyes which see the selves from which they have become alienated. They view themselves from the outside, in their alienation from the person they appear to be, becoming aware that their self is something different from their social self. In its perspective this self is more durable, one with a history of acts which it must and can call its own, one that has continuity and unity. They recognize that they are incarnate and exist in time, that they are their bodies. The creative powers which these characters engage are used to create themselves and to see with others' eyes.

The self-definition they attain does not represent a re-integration of the self they lost. They remain fragmented in a way which Kleist finds quite proper. For the Graf, the Prince, Julietta, and Toni, the self which is, in some sense, guilty -- the self which is and remains alien to them -- nevertheless is accepted as a moral part of what they are. It is precisely in the acceptance of that attachment that they transcend the self which they had wanted so desperately to disown.

This is the freedom which Kleist grants them. Before they arrived at this freedom through this peculiar type of transcendence, however -- and this is true for the way in which many other characters try to exist -- they had lived in a type of void which does not represent true freedom. The tendency of some to withdraw, to avoid existing, to avoid risks by ignoring or altering their experience when they are threatened, to retreat to the seemingly secure realm of play, to slip out of space and time, to destroy others, or even, as in the cases of Johann and Penthesilea, to destroy oneself, are all ways of being that are obviously not ways of genuinely existing. It is an attempt at freedom that does not represent any genuine freedom.

The characters who come to themselves are not non-entities nor do they feel the need to kill the subjectivity of others. They do not retreat, but rather they open themselves to the world and to others, aware of their selves in the light of others' consciousness. They do not try to make the world their own by denying, through self-delusion and the delusion and control of others, that the world and others have a validity that is independent of their own experience. The consciousness they gain is one of themselves and of others, not an absolute consciousness such as is described in the "Marionettentheater" as the goal of man's developing awareness, a consciousness that is infinite. In Kleist's creative works he shows himself to be much more interested in how individuals can be human than in what it means to be like a god.

It is thus not only in Kleist's depiction of the relativity of reality that he sets himself apart from German Classicism, but also in his depiction of the relativity of the self. The reality he sees is neither a reality of things nor a reality of the mind but rather a relationship between the two that denies an absolute quality to both. While Kleist grants an enormous power to the subjectivity of man, a capacity which indeed distinguishes man from the stable concreteness of natural laws and the order of natural forces, this power potentially can restrict and delude man rather than free him. Kleist is far from embracing a radical idealism that would allow, even subjectively, a transcendence of the real contexts of physical reality and of the presence of others.

Kleist has in this regard a closer affinity to the later Romantics who criticize the apotheosis of the self in early Romanticism and the lack of context which that implied. Those of

Kleist's characters who flee the reality around them for the supposed greener fields of the mind are not at all unlike Klara and Heinrich in Tieck's "Des Lebens Überfluß" of 1837, for example, who withdraw without provisions to an idyllic and hermetic retreat of the mind, confident that they can nourish each other with their love and their dreams, only to end up slowly burning up the stairs leading to the outside world in order to keep warm. In Kleist's works as here, there is an enormous tension and discrepancy between the powers of the mind with which individuals are endowed and the necessity to be in the world, between the inner world and the outer. Kleist is far more of a realist than he often is given credit for, although his interest is not in social reality on a large scale but in the reality which comes into being between and through the subjectivities of individuals who willy nilly must share a world. Kleist is a psychological realist, but this in the sense of being interested in the psychology of individuals, in the workings of their minds as they experience what impinges on them.

As a final and qualifying consideration, although Kleist's interest is basically a moral and an existential one, there is a sociological dimension to this set of problems as well. The minimal moral "ought" of Existentialism that is suggested, that one cannot be only for oneself but must also be for others, is developed by Kleist in its political dimension at least in a limited fashion. Tracing development of ideas in Kleist's works is nearly impossible because of the very brief time span of his creative life, some ten years, and because the time between conception and completion of several of his works spans a good part of that decade, but it is still possible to note an increasing interest in the nature of the state.

The problem of how the individual can come to a relationship with others, forming a "we," is a theme running throughout his ouevre, but the perspective appears to broaden in several works. Kohlhaas, in the novella begun in 1805, an individual, usurps the function of the creator of the law with dazzling effectiveness, and he does it for basically personal reasons. He becomes a leader of men and the figurehead for the attempted creation of a new order of political reality, but his vision is in fact not one of a new state. Nevertheless, the possibility of a visionary with the power to transform the thought and self-conception of a nation is introduced.

This occurs in fact in Hermannsschlacht. The problematic nature of Hermann's actions on an interpersonal level has been broached in earlier portions of this study, and the question of whether the end justifies the means is a problematic question on a different level, but there is one positive aspect of Hermann's manipulations which is of interest here. Hermann's manipulations lead to the formation of a new political world, an enormous creative act of the imagination that sets him far above the limited vision of the other characters in the play. In this political regard -- and especially given the contemporary events to which they have a reference -- the use to which he puts his imagination is from Kleist's point of view a thoroughly praiseworthy one. He accomplishes on the level of the nation a transformation that many individuals in Kleist's other works cannot accomplish with their own experience or with the experience of one other person. Hermann in essence transforms the consciousness of what the state is. He brings something into being which has not existed before, altering the status quo in which other characters in the play are stuck. In fact, it is precisely because his vision -- of something which is not yet there -- is so solid that his manipulations are so successful. He sees through the mechanism of how everyone around him thinks because he himself has gone beyond it.

Homburg represents yet a further step. Here the state as a political order already exists, and the issue becomes the moral nature of the state. Homburg comes to recognize, as does the Elector, that the state is a living entity that exists and continually comes into being through its members. The aspect of reality described earlier in more general terms, that what is real is real only because it exists in the experience of individuals, comes into play here. Both the Elector and Homburg recognize in the end the validity of the idea that the state's existence, like an individual's, relies on the experience of people for its essence, and that the state must be continually confirmed by the people who comprise it, or it will cease to exist. If the final line of the play, "In Staub mit allen Feinden Brandenburgs!" is not there simply because of Kleist's hope of impressing Princess Amalie, these considerations might well help to explain on a literary level what otherwise might seem to be an unmotivated statement.

Chapter 1. MIND AND REALITY

1. "Gebrechliche Welt" is a concept which figures prominently in
the work of Benno von Wiese, Die Deutsche Tragödie von
Lessing bis Hebbel, vol. 2 (Hamburg: Hoffmann und Campe,
1948), 15-102; of Paul Böckmann, "Die Verrätselung des
Daseins in Kleists Dichten," in Formensprache: Studien zur
Literarästhetik und Dichtungsinterpretationen (Hamburg:
Hoffman und Campe, 1966), 385-406; of Ingrid Kohrs, Das Wesen
des Tragischen im Drama Heinrichs von Kleist: Dargestellt an
Interpretationen von "Penthesilea" und "Prinz Friedrich von
Homburg" (Marburg/Lahn: Simons Verlag, 1951); and of Raimund
Belgardt, "Kleists Weg zur Wahrheit: Irrtum und Wahrheit als
Denkformen und Strukturmöglichkeiten," Zeitschrift für
Deutsche Philologie, 92 (1973), 161-184.

2. Gerhard Fricke develops the argument for feeling as an organ
of knowledge, especially in Gefühl und Schicksal bei
Heinrich von Kleist (Berlin: Junker und Dünnhaupt, 1929);
Dieter Harlos discusses the collision between feeling, which
he sees as an idealized image which Kleist's female
characters bring to bear on the male characters, and
understanding, the organ that perceives the real world, Die
Gestaltung psychischer Konflikte einiger Frauengestalten im
Werk Heinrich von Kleists (Frankfurt am Main: Peter Lang,
1984); Bohdan Bochan develops a more refined argument by
asserting that emotion is endowed with a cognitive power and
that feeling is a combination of emotion and reason, The
Phenomenology of Freedom in Kleist's "Die Familie
Schroffenstein" and "Penthesilea" (Frankfurt am Main: Peter
Lang, 1982); Hermann J. Weigand discusses trust in his
essays "Das Vertrauen als Zentralbegriff in Heinrich von
Kleists Dramatik" and "Das Vertrauen in Kleists Erzählungen,"
both in Fährten und Funde: Aufsätze zur Deutschen Literatur
(Bern: Francke, 1967), 72-84 and 85-119, respectively; Curt
Hohoff discusses knowing through dreaming in "Traum und
Wirklichkeit bei Heinrich von Kleist," Merkur, 15 (1961),
1026-1034; Gert Ueding also sees the dream as a central way
of experiencing the world and correctly notes the efficacy of
dream images in influencing the mind and reality in
"Zweideutige Bilderwelt: 'Das Käthchen von Heilbronn,'" in
Kleists Dramen: Neue Interpretationen (Stuttgart: Reclam,
1981), 52-72; Roland Heine, much as Hohoff, sees the dream as
the only access to certainty, although his argument also
notes that dreaming is a fictional form of reality and is not
a transcendental form of knowledge as it is for other

Romantics: "'Ein Traum, was sonst?': Zum Verhältnis von Traum und Wirklichkeit in Kleists 'Prinz Friedrich von Homburg,'" in Literaturwissenschaft und Geistesgeschichte: Festschrift für Richard Brinkman, ed. Jürgen Brummack et. al. (Tübingen: Max Niemeyer, 1981), 283-313; Klaus Müller-Salget includes a discussion of understanding in "Das Prinzip der Doppeldeutigkeit in Kleists Erzählungen," Zeitschrift für Deutsche Philologie, 92 (1973), 185-211; autonomous self-consciousness is a cornerstone of Friedrich Koch's excellent study, Heinrich von Kleist: Bewußtsein und Wirklichkeit (Stuttgart: Metzler and Carl Ernst Poeschel, 1958).

3. Ernst Cassirer discusses the possibility that Kleist was really referring to the philosophy of Fichte. Heinrich von Kleist und die Kantische Philosophie (Berlin: Reuther & Reichard, 1919).

4. All citations from Kleist's works are from Sämtliche Werke und Briefe, ed. Helmut Sembdner, 6th ed. (Munich: Hanser Verlag, 1977). For the reader's ease of reference, citations from the letters, variants, or prose works (vol. 2) are indicated by a page reference given in parentheses following the citation. Line numbers for the citations from the dramas (vol. 1) are given in parentheses following the citation.

5. It is useful to distinguish between consciousness as psychic activity of the subject and other possible definitions of consciousness which equate it with identity. Koch clearly uses such a definition as the latter in Bewußtsein und Wirklichkeit, where consciousness means an absolute knowledge of one's own self that collides with reality. The first nine chapters of this study deal primarily with consciousness as the activity of the mind; the final three with the question of identity.

6. Linda Dietrick, in Prisons and Idylls: Studies in Heinrich von Kleist's Fictional Worlds (Frankfurt: Peter Lang, 1985), centers the development of her arguments on the observation that the issue is subjectivity and consciousness, not knowledge. By beginning with a flexible definition of consciousness as a mental working-through of reality, Dietrick argues that meaning is disclosed only through the world as experienced, a world shaped by interpretation. While noting that perspective is thus of prime importance, she nonetheless sees subjectivity as a hindrance to the complete apprehension of "true" reality and sees consciousness as a matter of boundaries rather than as an essentially human way in which the interpersonal dynamics among Kleist's characters unfold, 8, 198.

7. See also Cassirer, Kleist und die Kantische Philosophie.

8. Ilse Graham limits herself somewhat in this fashion in her argument that Kleist sought a way of knowing that is

unmediated by the senses, Heinrich von Kleist: Word into
Flesh: A Poet's Quest for the Symbol (Berlin, New York: de
Gruyter, 1977).

9. Walter Müller-Seidel brought the term Versehen into general
usage in Kleist criticism, Versehen und Erkennen: Eine
Studie über Heinrich von Kleist (Cologne: Böhlau, 1961).
The term has remained attached to Müller-Seidel, although he
himself says that the real problem lies in the discrepancy
between not knowing and consciousness. With that, he shows
himself to be precisely in the tradition of Gerhard Fricke,
and in fact Müller-Seidel is a staunch defender of the
concept of absolute feeling as Kleist's alternative means of
knowing. The result is that he engages very little in
examining the minds of the characters as individual entities,
relegating in fact the minds of secondary characters to a
"typische Denkweise." Koch, though claiming that Gefühl
should not be used as a basis for discussing Kleist, chooses
a dichotomy between consciousness and reality, but since he
conceives of consciousness as a monolithic and absolute
entity, this is in practice just another name for what Fricke
called feeling. Psychology implicitly or explicitly is often
rejected when dealing with such absolutes. Hermann J.
Weigand is a classic example of this, "Das Vertrauen als
Zentralbegriff in Heinrich von Kleists Dramatik," also "Das
Vertrauen in Kleists Erzählungen," where the use of
psychology as a means to approach Kleist's characters is
considered superfluous and unworkable.

10. Karl Otto Conrady, "Das Moralische in Kleists Erzählungen:
Ein Kapitel vom Dichter ohne Gesellschaft," in Literatur und
Gesellschaft: vom neunzehnten ins zwanzigste Jahrhundert:
Festschrift für Benno von Wiese, ed. Hans Joachim Schrimpf
(Bonn: Bouvier, 1963). More recently, Bohdan Bochan has
argued that man is thrown by Kleist into abysmal situations
and that it is here that man molds his responses, simultaneously a participant and a creator of events from which
there is no escape except through the situation, The
Phenomenology of Freedom, 26. Bochan also does not see
freedom as a transcendental issue. The minds of Kleist's
characters, with their conscious and subconscious desires and
needs, have begun to be the focus of some recent studies, and
such critics as James M. McGlathery take Kleist criticism to
task for its preoccupation with a search for transcendental
meaning, Desire's Sway. The Plays and Stories of Heinrich
von Kleist (Detroit: Wayne State University Press, 1983).

11. In the "Verlobung" some other examples are such descriptions
as that of Toni's "schöne Seele"(193), which could be a
response generated by anyone present at her death,
substantivized adjectives such as "der Unglückliche," which
reflects Toni's attitude to Gustav, and nouns containing a
subjective dimension of judgment that may be objectively
suspect, such as the description of Gustav as Toni's

"friend"(185). This is not restricted to the "Verlobung," however. Beat Beckmann painstakingly documents shifts in perspective in some of Kleist's novellas to demonstrate where the narrator would have to be in order to see or to know what he is relating. Kleists Bewußtseinskritik: Eine Untersuchung der Erzählform seiner Novellen (Bern: Peter Lang, 1978). My study focuses on the way characters cope with their world and on ways to think about a pattern of Kleist's concerns, but his novellas can indeed be examined through an inquiry into the question of the reliability of the narrator. The reliability, or rather the unreliability, of the narrators has been developed by other critics, most compellingly by John Ellis, who points out that the narrative voice in the novellas does not serve to clarify events, but distorts or obscures them, both by what is added and by what is left out. John Ellis sees this, rightly I think, as an invitation to the reader to go in search of the facts through examination of peripheral information. Heinrich von Kleist: Studies in the Character and Meaning of his Writings (Chapel Hill: University of North Carolina Press, 1979). This argument has been developed most thoroughly in treatments of Kleist's "Findling." Erna Moore also interprets this novella through the events of story rather than through the narration in "Heinrich von Kleists 'Findling': Psychologie des Verhängnisses," Colloquia Germanica, 1974, 275-297. Marjorie Gelus examines the contribution of the narrative voice in rendering uncanny the environment presented in the "Findling." "Displacement of Meaning: Kleist's 'Der Findling,'" German Quarterly, 55 (1982), 541-55. Axel Laurs also comments on the absence of a conventional authorial presence and the uneasy overlapping introduction of new perspectives, "Narrative Strategy in Heinrich von Kleist's 'Die Heilige Cäcilie oder Die Gewalt der Musik (Eine Legende),'" Journal of the Australasian Universities Language and Literature Association, 60 (198), 220-233. Linda Dietrick observes that the narrator undermines the authority of his perspective by not maintaining a wide and consistent point of view, Prisons and Idylls, 9.

Chapter 2. LANGUAGE AS ENVIRONMENT: THE BOUNDARIES OF CONSCIOUSNESS

1. Hans Heinz Holz, Macht und Ohnmacht der Sprache: Unter-suchungen zum Sprachverständnis und Stil Heinrich von Kleists (Frankfurt am Main: Athenäum, 1962), 23. He also refers to Kleist's words as showing the tragedy of misunderstanding, 107.

2. Holz believes that reason finds its instrument in language, 85. Müller-Seidel takes this position as well, "Die Struktur des Widerspruchs in Kleists 'Marquise von O...,'" Deutsche

Vierteljahresschrift für Literaturwissenschaft und Geistesgeschichte, 28 (1954), 502, and he sees language as the "Mittel des Verstandes" which is caught up in the world of appearances.

3. Holz, *Ibid.* 24, and Müller-Seidel, *Ibid.* Günther Blöcker also argues that the true person is ineffable for similar reasons, *Heinrich von Kleist oder das Absolute Ich* (Berlin: Argon, 1960).

4. Thus Holz, *Ibid.*, 59.

5. Sosias' comic speech is based on Moliere's Sosias, of course, but that does not preclude noting Kleist's fascination with this sort of linguistic illusion.

6. This has been argued recently and cogently by other critics as well. Linda Dietrick sees the concept of space in Kleist's works as one of figurative as well as concrete significance, and she notes language as the space in which meaning unfolds and argues for the powerful organizational function of language, *Prisons and Idylls*, 3. Also Anthony Stephens, in an excellent recent article, sees that language in Kleist's works has the tendency to become self-referential and that language appears to be able to bend reality in any way it will, "The Illusion of a Shaped World: Kleist and Tragedy," *Journal of the Australasian Universities Language and Literature Association*, 60, Nov. 1983, 205.

7. It is interesting to note, however, that one aspect of the speech of Kleist's characters is not an issue here. All of the characters in a given work speak at a uniform level of style, regardless of whatever differences exist in content and metaphorical usage. Differences in the plane of style which are so significant in much of the literature of the 19th century are never an aspect of communication or of misunderstanding here.

8. One is reminded of a similar scene in Büchner's *Danton's Tod* where Lucille performs one of the most effortless suicides in German literature. She walks into the plaza and shouts, "Es lebe der König!" While the similarity of historical situations is coincidental, the similarity of concerns is not. Both Büchner and Kleist are profoundly concerned with language and how one is who one is.

9. Hinrich Seeba correctly points out that the enmity between the houses becomes a timeless institution which fills the characters' consciousness. He is also quite correct when he inserts that *Schroffenstein* was conceived of as a *Sprachtragödie*. "Der Sündenfall des Verdachts: Identitätskrise und Sprachskepsis in Kleists 'Familie Schroffenstein,'" *Deutsche Vierteljahresschrift für Literaturwissenschaft und Geistesgeschichte*, 44 (1970), 72, 78. Seeba also draws

attention to the fact that in this drama it is not reality
that is at issue but language, through which reality has
already been interpreted and thus fixed. Stephens also sees
human structuring in the drama, stating that the tragic
blindness "is based not so much on the fact that an
individual's perspective is necessarily limited but rather
that it is over-structured." In the same vein he points out
that the human misperceptions of reality are "so destructive
that the tricks of Fate which set the action going become
well-nigh superfluous." "Illusion of a Shaped World," 203,
206.

10. Gerhard Kluge also notes the perversion of nature and the way
in which Rupert's and Sylvester's language and positions
change places, although Kluge sees this as arising from man's
incapacity to understand the world around him. "Der Wandel
der dramatischen Konzeption von der 'Familie Ghonorez' zur
'Familie Schroffenstein,'" in Kleists Dramen: Neue
Interpretationen, 52-72.

11. In treating the problem of questioning in Kleist's works,
Günther Blöcker develops an argument from a related but
different angle, stating that it is the questioning which is
important, not the answer, that confronted with the
unknowable, man becomes conscious of himself and creates
himself through asking. Das Absolute Ich, esp. 140-142. For
Blöcker as well as for Kommerell, who also treats the topic
of interrogation, the impossibility of solving the problem of
the puzzle of man through questioning looms large. Man is
ineffable. "Die Sprache und das Unaussprechliche: Eine
Betrachtung über Heinrich von Kleist," in Geist und Buchstabe
der Dichtung: Goethe, Schiller, Kleist, Hölderlin, 4th
edition (Frankfurt: Klostermann, 1956), esp. 247ff. Seeba,
"Der Sündenfall des Verdachts," based in some measure on
Kommerell, advances the argument that the examinations do not
serve the revelation of truth but rather confuse and obscure
it, esp. 432f.

12. Anthony Stephens discusses the nature of this inquisition and
others in Kleist's works and sees the nature of power
relationships as being at the core of their structure: he
sees the "Erzählung als <syntagmatische> Machtausübung in der
Sprache gegenüber den paradigmatischen Machtinstanzen, die
die jeweilige dramatische Situation bestimmen." "'Was
hilfts, dass ich jetzt schuldlos mich erzähle?': Zur
Bedeutung der Erzählvorgänge in Kleists Dramen," Jahrbuch
der Deutschen Schillergesellschaft, 29 (1985), 301.
Stephen's argument is persuasive in its dynamics, although in
this case Stephens believes that Theobald is more conscious
in his attempts to assert power through his control of
testimony than I have argued.

13. Oskar Seidlin discusses this problem of simultaneity in "What
the Bell Tolls in Kleist's Der Zerbrochene Krug," Deutsche

Vierteljahresschrift für Literaturwissenschaft und Geistesgeschichte, 51 (1977), 78-97. Seidlin is primarily interested in the numerical significance of the eleventh hour,
however, rather than in the epistemological problems presented by this paradox.

Chapter 3. THE CONTROL OF REALITY

1. Friedrich Koch is the only other critic to take note of this
important scene, although he bypasses the intense battle that
Sylvester is waging for order and for his very sense of
order. Koch believes Sylvester cannot comprehend the
magnitude and content of Aldöbern's accusation and covers his
"Verlegenheit" by suggesting Aldöbern sit down. Koch is
quite correct in seeing the power of the final accusation as
being instrumental in the breakdown of Sylvester's
consciousness, however. Bewußtsein und Wirklichkeit, 64.

2. Koch also notes the peculiar absence of comment on the actual
murder. He is quite correct in stating, "die Wirklichkeit
wird gar nicht als Maßstab für die Wahrheit des Bewußtseins
angerufen." Bewußtsein und Wirklichkeit, 67. Characteristic
for Koch is to view consciousness as content rather than as a
structure, a system of fragments of conscious activity that
engage in both knowing and being. Noting the threat to
Sylvester's consciousness, Koch concludes that Sylvester is
defending a subjective truth which he holds for absolute
against a different subjective truth which Aldöbern holds for
absolute. It seems to be, rather, that Sylvester's
consciousness is very much in active motion here: he is
willing to shift any aspect of reality in this battle for
control of the flow of reality, in order to prevent damage to
his self by becoming fixed as a murderer. Sylvester's world
is hardly held for absolute; he is the weaker of the two in
this scene and is defensive from the outset. His control of
self and reality is weak, and not merely because Aldöbern is
so sure of himself, as we saw earlier in the discussion where
Sylvester is seen to experience and acknowledge a shift in
his world and reality. It is perhaps also an overstatement
to say that Aldöbern is holding a reality for absolute. He
is the bearer of a message -- delivered verbatim and
infinitely repeatable.

3. V.C. Hubbs, on the other hand, in "Die Romantische Mythe der
Transformation," in Husbanding the Golden Grain: Studies in
Honor of Henry W. Nordmeyer, ed. Luanne T. Frank and Emery E.
George (Ann Arbor: University of Michigan (Edwards Brothers),
1973), takes Sylvester's collapse into unconsciousness as a
retreat to the core of his being, from which he awakens
refreshed, 173. Sylvester may change, but hardly for the
better.

216

Chapter 4. NAMING AND KNOWLEDGE: THE REDUCTION OF PHENOMENA

1.   Robert Labhardt, in his sensitive study, Metapher und
      Geschichte: Kleists dramatische Metaphorik bis zur
      'Penthesilea' als Widerspiegelung seiner geschichtlichen
      Position (Kronberg/Ts.: Scriptor, 1976), examines the use of
      metaphor in Kleist's works extensively and likewise sees
      Rupert's speech as an associative progression towards a form
      of knowledge of reality: "Das Bildbereich entwickelt syntag-
      matisch seine eigene Logik und substituiert sie als Hand-
      lungsanweisung dem realen Sachverhalt. Rupert legitimiert
      seine Absichten mit bildlicher Suggestion, nicht durch
      Rationalität," 105. He sees that the hyperbole is in fact an
      indication that Rupert is trying to triumph over reality by
      replacing the grounds of justification with emotionality and
      by subordinating the objective world to the subjective, 117f.
      Lilian Hoverland, in her excellent book, also sees in
      Kleist's works a tendency towards an "Ent-Realisierung" of
      narrated occurrences and towards a "Verselbstständigung der
      Sprache," Heinrich von Kleist und das Prinzip der Gestaltung
      (Königstein/Ts.: Scriptor, 1979), 23. Hoverland argues that
      reality is re-formed and transformed in the imagination in
      order to restore order to the multiplicity and ambiguity of
      appearances. She sees such psychic activity in most cases as
      a passively negating activity directed against phenomena,
      however, rather than as an aggressive movement into the
      environment that affects others. Hoverland bases her
      argument here on a rupture, rather than a social confluence,
      between self and world in Kleist's works, as does Labhardt,
      who sees at root a tragic antinomy of self and world in
      Kleist's works due to and reflecting Kleist's sense of social
      isolation and his desire for the ideal of a unity between a
      natural feudalism and a humane society, 159.

2.   Cf. also "europäische Hunde"(186) and "weiße und kreolische
      Halbhunde"(166).

3.   Cf. also "Gattung"(177) and "Geschlecht"(191) as manifesta-
      tions of the we-they division of humanity. Toni, neither
      black nor white, is the character in the middle whom the
      other characters attempt to get to think as they do.

4.   It is because she is not fixable within the boundaries of his
      past experience that he needs the name. She is a "Glanz-
      erscheinung"(1809), literally "<die> Unbegreifliche"(1811),
      and the name would provide the handle with which to begin to
      grasp her. Thus he asks who she is: "Wie nenn ich dich,
      wenn meine eigene Seele sich, die entzückte, fragt, wem sie
      gehört?" (1812-13) An unfortunate choice of words on his
      part, for she does want to own him. His speech, as elsewhere
      in the play, is formulaic here and does not operate on the
      same level as the one on which it is received by Penthesilea.
      He of course does not mean that he in fact belongs to her.

Penthesilea, on the other hand, cannot sense irony because she cannot exist on two linguistic levels at once. Cf. 1. 1611, when she has asked whether it is true that she has captured him; he answers, "In jedem schönren Sinn, erhabne Königin!" That sort of dual perspective is something of which she is incapable.

5. It may be ironic, but not entirely unexpected. She cannot be gentle in his presence because he threatens her in very basic ways by his mere proximity. See chapters 10 and 11.

6. Sander L. Gilman, in his article on the aesthetics of blackness in the novella, points out that Gustav thinks and observes according to a destructively rigid perspectivism of black-white aesthetics which impairs ethical judgment when used as a way to view others and the world. Gilman bypasses, however, the social-historical setting and the process through which Gustav, and others in the novella, come to think this way. "The Aesthetics of Blackness in Heinrich von Kleist's 'Die Verlobung in St. Domingo,'" MLN, 90 (1975), 661-2. He also argues that Gustav transforms Toni into a white, but Gilman sees this as the result of Gustav's prejudiced and limited perception and as the result of Gustav's identification of her with the forces of good, 670. Lilian Hoverland, building on Gilman, also believes that Gustav's treatment of Toni is really a "Versagung" and that his suicide represents atonement for Toni's, and Mariane's, deaths. Hoverland sees the dynamics of the story as the "Problematik der Augen, die die Wirklichkeit nicht wahrzunehmen fähig sind." Heinrich von Kleist und das Prinzip der Gestaltung, 154-159.

7. Hoverland, who notes that Gustav does not see Mariane with any complexity at all, sees a religious parallel of an inter-esting and very different sort. Hoverland draws a parallel between Mariane's turning away from Gustav and Peter's denial of Christ and sees in this gesture anger at Gustav's betrayal of her by leaving her behind when he fled to the suburbs of Paris, Das Prinzip der Gestaltung, 154, 156. Given the way Gustav's mind works, this is, clearly, entirely possible, but I am not inclined to doubt the purity of Mariane's sacrifice for structural reasons: her "denial" is parallel to Toni's selfless, sacrificial "denial" of Gustav.

8. "... inzwischen sah er soviel ein, daß er gerettet, und in dem Hause, in welchem er sich befand, für ihn nichts von dem Mädchen zu befürchten war"(175).

Chapter 5. THE CONTROL OF TRUTH

1. J. Huizinga, Homo Ludens: A Study of the Play-Element in Culture (London: Routledge & Kegan, Ltd., 1949).

2. The existential problem of play as a way of existing is taken up in the chapter 7. Word games are of interest there, too, of course. But the choice of such terms as delusion and collusion is not based in this chapter on existential role considerations. Also, such terms are workable for normal relationships, both social and personal. The terms are used in part by Huizinga, also by Erving Goffman in The Presentation of Self in Everyday Life (New York: Doubleday Anchor, 1959), and in Where the Action Is (London: Allen Lane, The Penguin Press, 1969), esp. 37-206. The current discussion aims to delineate the epistemological and ontological problems in Kleist's works. The terms as used by R.D. Laing in Self and Others (London: Tavistock, 1969) revolve around quandary and pathology rather than normality and are thus more appropriate here. I am beholden to Laing's discussion of elusion, 32ff., and to his whole discussion of the breakdown of the relationship between self and other in pathological cases.

3. Ilse Graham sees the exchange of clothing as a sign of their total trust, a symbolic token of their being transparent to one another, Word into Flesh, 51. Obviously, Ottokar is not being open with her, however, regardless of his motives.

4. Cf. also his command to his wife: "tu mir den Gefallen und schweig! ... Es ist mir verhaßt, wenn ich nur davon höre" (132).

5. Holz refers to the "Tragödie des Geistes, der vergeblich im Wort der Wirklichkeit zu entrinnen sucht." In noting this magical power of the word in connection with his discussion of Guiskard and others of Kleist's characters, Holz calls it the "tiefmythische Beziehung zwischen Sprache, Wahrheit, und Wirklichkeit," Macht und Ohnmacht, 46.

6. See also 139. The mother terminates the apology scene between father and daughter and restores the familial order by means of a joke: "Sie rief: o was für ein Gesicht ist das! ... und machte der Rührung durch Scherzen ein Ende. Sie lud und führte beide ... zur Abendtafel ...." Marjorie Gelus discusses this scene in a similar vein, "Laughter and Joking in the Works of Heinrich von Kleist, German Quarterly, 90 (1977), 452-473.

7. Henry Rottenbiller, as later do Labhardt (Metapher und Geschichte) and Stephens ("Illusion of a Shaped World"), also argues that the source and reference points of the metaphor in Kleist's works frequently lie totally within the

mind of a character. "Die Metaphorik der Psychogenen Kausalität in den Dichtungen Heinrich von Kleists," Diss. Michigan State University, 1971. See <u>DA</u> 32, No. 3-4 (1971), 1527A.

8. Bochan's book revolves in large measure around the question of the abdication of self-responsibility and one's own freedom. In his discussion of the use of language in the play, he makes the interesting observations that "the protagonists exist in and through idle talk," and that "freedom is unattainable, not because of 'Zufall,' but because the protagonists have entrusted themselves to the jurisdiction of the 'they' from the outset," <u>The Phenomenology of Freedom</u>, 86, 92.

9. Cf. 167, 168, 169, 172 (2x), 173 (2x), 175 (2x), 181.

Chapter 6. THE AUTONOMY OF SELF AND REALITY

1. Dorrit Cohn in "Kleist's 'Marquise von O...': The Problem of Knowledge." <u>Monatshefte</u>, 67 (1975), 142.

2. Hohoff sees Kleist's world view as one of chaos and catastrophe, <u>Komik und Humor bei Heinrich von Kleist: Ein Beitrag zur Klärung der geistigen Struktur eines Dichters</u>, <u>Germanische Studien</u>, pt. 184, 1937, 118. Also Helbling, who describes the depicted reality as chaotic and impenetrable, <u>The Major Works of Heinrich von Kleist</u> (New York: New Directions, 1975), 50. Durzak sees a "Katastrophensituation als Weltbild" confronting the moral power which resides in the heart, "Zur Utopischen Funktion des Kindesbildes in Kleists Erzählungen," <u>Colloquia Germanica</u>, 1969, 118. "Gebrechliche Welt" is the favorite term for the destructive power of reality; it is notably employed by Hans Joachim Schrimpf, "Der Zerbrochne Krug," in <u>Das Deutsche Drama vom Barock bis zur Gegenwart</u>, vol. 1, ed. Benno von Wiese (Düsseldorf: August Bagel, 1958), 339. See also above, p. 3. Hans Peter Hermann believes coincidence gets raised to the law of reality and becomes fate, "Zufall und Ich: Zum Begriff der Situation in den Novellen Heinrich von Kleists," <u>Germanisch-Romanische Monatsschrift</u>, NS 11 (1961), 90; similarly Ernst Fischer in his essay, "Heinrich von Kleist," in <u>Heinrich von Kleist: Aufsätze und Essays</u>, ed. Walter Müller-Seidel (Darmstadt: Wissenschaftliche Buchgesellschaft, 1973), 482, and Karlheinz Stierle in "Das Beben des Bewußtseins: Die narrative Struktur von Kleists 'Das Erdbeben in Chili,'" in <u>Positionen der Literaturwissenschaft: Acht Modellanalysen am Beispiel von Kleists "Das Erdbeben in Chili</u>," ed. David E. Wellbery (München: Beck, 1985), 54-68; Joachim Müller notes coincidence, but does not see it as determinism, at least for Nicolo in "Der Findling," who uses

every coincidence to exploit a situation for his personal gain, "Zufall und Vorfall: Geschehenswelt und Erzählstruktur in Heinrich von Kleists Novelle Der Findling," Zeitschrift für Germanistik, 4 (1982), 427-438. In a different direction on a similar topic, however, Norbert Altenhofer discusses "das Rätselhafte" and views it not as a factual but as a hermeneutic event which leads to a questioning of natural, social, and metaphysical ordering, "Der erschütterte Sinn: Hermeneutische Überlegungen zu Kleists 'Das Erdbeben in Chili,'" in Positionen der Literaturwissenschaft, 39-53.

3. Even Schroffenstein, written as the fate tragedies were coming into vogue, avoids that imposition of external control. One of Kleist's marginal notes to IV, 3 of the Familie Ghonerez indicates that the thought had occurred to him at least: "Man könnte eine Hexe aufführen, die wirklich das Schicksal gelenkt hätte"(833). He rejects that, however, and he also drops the suggestive word "Püppchen" as a reference to the characters in the closing scene to assist in the removal of the notion that the characters were not responsible for their acts. Rupert, of course, picks up on the idea, but he has himself established a pattern of avoidance of moral responsibility for his acts.

4. John Ellis sees the whip as a sign of Piachi's menacing attitude towards everyone in the house. Heinrich von Kleist: Studies in the Character and Meaning of his Writings (Chapel Hill: University of North Carolina, 1979), 17.

5. Rene Girard argues in a different direction on this question. He sees the deaths of Jeronimo and Josephe as a ritual sacrifice which is required to restore social order. The "sacrifice" obliterates the past event of the earthquake and makes it possible for the mob to change God from an evil god back into a good god. "Mythos und Gegenmythos: Zu Kleists 'Das Erdbeben in Chili,'" in Positionen der Literaturwissenschaft, 130-148. Even in this argument, however, it is man who ultimately "controls" what God is to be by ritualistically determining God's moral essence. The presence of rituals in Kleist's works, formalized ways of organizing and dealing with reality, is a topic which still remains to be explored systematically.

6. As the discussion of the self-deceptive aspects of this issue revealed, there is no question here of an actual transcendental possibility of consciousness: Kleist's characters are not allowed to live in their imagination, at least not for very long. Kleist drags his characters through the abusive realities of social and physical contexts and destroys that dimension of idealistic transcendence.

7. Criticism has generally focused on the individual rather than the contest. E. L. Stahl is one exception, pointing out the absence of a lyric quality in Kleist's works, a lyric quality

one can find in a _Hamlet_ or an _Iphigenia_: "He presented characters in conflict not with themselves, but with others. Their attention is fixed on the minds and the actions of their partners and their adversaries ...," in _Heinrich von Kleist's Dramas_ (Oxford: Blackwell, 1948), 24. Somewhat in the tradition of Gundolf, Stahl sees the conflicts as being the result of the exalted strength of human passion in the individual, unbridled by any reliable power of human reason or human feelings, see 19f, 51f. Müller-Seidel likewise takes partial note of this in _Versehen und Erkennen_, where he argues that the environment of the characters is the characters themselves, that Kleist's heroes and heroines form their fate in the battle with that environment, 37. Müller-Seidel's study works for the most part in the arena of social conflict rather than experience, which results in the reduction of all but the main characters to societal roles, to what he calls a "typische Denkweise," _Ibid._ and throughout. The subjectivity of others is largely not a source of interest to his study.

Chapter 7. THE MANIPULATION OF THE OTHER: ROLES AND ROLE MODELS

1. Lilian Hoverland also makes this point for Penthesilea, although her argument is an epistemological one rather than an existential one, _Das Prinip der Gestaltung_, 79. Bohdan Bochan, however, argues precisely in this phenomenological manner when he says that her love negates the freedom of the other by turning the other into an object, _The Phenomenology of Freedom_, 123.

2. Sven Olaf Hoffmann in his psychoanalytic study also sees this incorporation as a combination of destruction and preservation of Achilles. Hoffmann associates the biting into the left breast of Achilles with a subconscious desire to castrate her father, Ares, who had robbed her of her breast, precipitating sexual insecurity. In so doing, Hoffmann continues, she regains her breast and her femininity and destroys and gains the masculinity of her father. "Das Identitätsproblem in Heinrich von Kleists _Penthesilea_," in _Psychoanalytische Textinterpretationen_, ed. Johannes Cremerius (Hamburg: Hoffmann und Campe, 1974), 172-180.

3. Friedrich Gundolf, _Heinrich von Kleist_ (Leipzig: Hesse und Becker, 1922), 115.

4. Fricke, _Gefühl und Schicksal_, 94. Similarly Hans Schwerte, who sees in that scene a harmonious consonance as the final chord of the play, "Das Käthchen von Heilbronn," _Der Deutschunterricht_, 13.2 (1961), 5-26. In viewing this scene it is interesting to take note of Franz Horn's comment in 1819 that Kleist felt dissatisfied with the last part of the

play and had planned to revise the ending and go on to add a second part to the play. According to Horn, in the reworked version Strahl wounds Käthchen through something he says and she flees him; as a result of the pain of losing her, Strahl reflects and achieves a higher moral worth, something lacking in the last scene as it stands, and they regain each other in a more genuinely harmonious ending, quoted by Sembdner in Kleist's _Werke_, 940.

5. Much in contradiction to this, Robert Labhardt sees Jeronimus as an impartial representative of the truth of the real world, while Johann is an uncompromising representative of the truth of the self. For these reasons Labhardt sees them both as good and as innocent. _Metapher und Geschichte_, 161.

6. One understands, in this light, why Gustav, in the "Verlobung," wonders what is in store for him when he is ushered into the dead Villeneuve's rooms and is told that this is where he belongs. His sense of forboding as he looks over that earlier scene of murder is readily understandable.

7. Erna Moore touches on this aspect in her article, "Heinrich von Kleists 'Findling': Psychologie des Verhängnisses" (_Colloquia Germanica_, 1974, 275-297). Moore points out that there are no complaints about Nicolo's behavior until he reaches puberty and attempts to go his own way; also, that Nicolo learns that he is rewarded precisely when he fulfills the expectations of his parents and that he learns to obey outwardly, esp. 281ff.

8. Sander Gilman sees the use of light and darkness as the key to Kleist's critique of the aesthetics of blackness, and he notes the way that Babekan and Toni create a masquerade which plays on Gustav's limited perception. "The Aesthetics of Blackness," 669.

9. A similar playing with Gustav is her reference to the blacks as "Räubergesindel"(165). It is, in fact, Babekan herself who is most interested in the property of others. When she devises the plan to have Gustav send a note to his people, it is not so much to capture the whites, but rather, she notes that the letter is important, "indem die Familie wahrscheinlich beträchtliche Habseligkeiten mit sich führe"(176). Toni, on the other hand, comes to view Babekan's and her actions as those of "Räuber"(177).

10. Gundolf develops the opposite viewpoint in his book, finding the basic impulse in Kleist's works coming from the characters' being possessed by wild and monomaniacal passions. Gundolf sees in the characters a blindness, a lack of power to order and form their environment, and their lives as resulting from uncontrollable emotions. _Heinrich von Kleist_, 340, 115 and throughout.

Chapter 8. THE SOCIAL SELF: THE ACTOR

1. These are two pillars of Ilse Graham's argument. These
    observations are quite true, of course, and these problems
    are seldom absent in Kleist's works, but one might well add
    that in the social context of interaction these problems are
    frequently results and symptoms, not the underlying causes
    for the lack of relatedness between individuals. Graham sees
    the basic impulse in Kleist's works arising out of a quest
    for absolute truth and does not treat those aspects of
    situations that deal with the beleaguered characters'
    attempts to get out of the scene and out of the work alive
    and intact. She stops at the problem of defective cognition
    and the common human plight of limitations. Even Kleist's
    characters do not blame their own flaws for their mistakes in
    judgment; they are all too often aware that others have been
    fooling them. Graham, Word into Flesh.

2. Curt Hohoff also sees this element of acting in Hermann. He
    also notices the affinity between Hermann's manipulative
    activities as ability to distance oneself from reality and
    from one's role in reality and the essential distancing
    quality of humor. Hohoff calls Hermann "the genuine
    humorist" who attempts to retain his unconditional and
    absolute position of freedom, rising and remaining above the
    human context. I might add that this is a definition of the
    actor who is conscious of acting. Komik und Humor, 56ff.

3. Of course, she is not dissembling in the "engagement scene,"
    but one can only speak in a very qualified manner about
    interaction in that scene.

4. These two selves are, of course, viewed by a third and
    dynamic self, the self as arbiter of acts, as governor of
    future deeds. It is this self, inseparable from a moral
    consciousness, that can free him from the deadlock in which
    he finds himself. This is an issue concerning the structure
    of the self. See below, chapters 11 and 12.

5. "Er trat duch eine Pforte, die er offen fand, in den
    Garten..."(128) Kleist is perhaps suggesting here that the
    violation of Julietta's personal space in this scene has a
    certain situational similarity to his violation of her in
    their first encounter.

6. Dorrit Cohn, in her article on the problem of knowledge in
    the "Marquise," properly draws attention to this scene; Cohn
    sees the Graf "intentionally casting himself in the role of a
    supernatural apparition," 137. Cohn's article develops the
    interaction from the perspective of Julietta and points out
    that the angelic or godlike quality of the Graf is totally
    within the fantasies of the Marquise herself, welling up out
    of the repressed depths of her psyche which does not want to

confront or acknowledge the physical and sexual reality of the Graf, 134, 132-3. One might add here that the Graf plays his role well and knows his audience in the Marquise, at least in this regard.

7. That Achilles does not wear his armor into battle with Penthesilea has another metaphorical function as well: it is a visual indication that he is not engaging in battle with Penthesilea as a warrior who intends to win; he is indicating his intention to be "vulnerable." Kleist is using one object, the armor, as the anchor of two metaphors. The second use does not work particularly well because Achilles appears somewhat silly going into battle without armor and armament: at the very least he ought to play his role in that drama in proper costume for the sake of credibility.

8. Aspects of Achilles' arrogance are noted by Weigand, who observes that Achilles only wants to possess Penthesilea and that he enters into the "battle" with her in blind faith that she will understand his galant gesture; he plays with and devalues her trust. Weigand goes so far as to state that Achilles' attitude removes him from the reader's sympathy and that the reader observes his death with relative coolness in comparison to Penthesilea's death, "Das Vertrauen als Zentralbegriff in Kleists Dramatik," 78-9. Kommerell in speaking of Achilles takes up a similar view: "<Achilles> verliert sich nicht an sie, er ist List und Stärke des Mannes und lachender Übermut des Bewußtseins," "Die Sprache und das Unaussprechliche," 275.

Chapter 9. FACADE AND INTERACTION

1. John Ellis also comments on the fact that the characters live in private worlds and that they play pro forma roles in the lives of the others. Studies, see esp. 6ff.

2. Erna Moore sees Elvire as the character who spreads the unhealthy atmosphere of secrecy, inaccessibility and silence in Piachi's house. "Psychologie des Verhängnisses, pp. 280ff."

3. See also his fear when in Elvire's chambers searching for her mysterious lover: "<es> ergriff ihn schon Furcht, von Elviren entdeckt und gestraft zu werden"(207, emphasis mine). Erna Moore also points out this aspect of Nicolo's duties to his step-parents, "Psychologie des Verhängnisses," 283-4. He closes the door and flees. Ellis speaks quite accurately of "how the needs of one person in a relationship dictate the role of the second, regardless of the appropriateness of the second to that role," Studies, 19.

Chapter 10. Private Worlds and Identity

1. Kunigunde might qualify as a villain, but she and the other characters in the drama are drawn so schematically that taking her as a real model for behavior would be overstating the evil in her nature.

2. Trying to draw out of the works a **proper** form of behavior for Kleist's characters is difficult, indeed. Klaus Müller-Salget, for example, says that in a fragile world man is dependent on the truthfulness of others, and man ought not deceive others in a world where experience is already ambiguous. Müller-Salget's conclusion that if only man maintained a solidarity of truthfulness with his fellow man, then things would work out better for Kleist's characters, oversimplifies the matter somewhat by tending to ignore the complexity of situation and of personality in Kleist's works. "Das Prinzip der Doppeldeutigkeit," 210-211. Müller-Salget is close to Weigand here, who believes that if only Kleist's characters trusted each other more, despite appearances, then things would work out better. See both of Weigand's essays in Fährten und Funde.

3. Curt Hohoff, "Traum und Wirklichkeit," esp. 1032.

4. This is basically an argument based on Idealism. Gerhard Fricke, Gefühl und Schicksal.

5. John Ellis has pointed out that Nicolo's relationship with Xaviera is a durable one, having continued for over five years at this point. Ellis interprets the relationship as one of beauty and love, standing in contrast to Piachi's and Elvire's diseased marriage. Not enough information is given within the story to conclude that the relationship between Nicolo and Xaviera is that unambiguously promising, although the suggestion of a positive relationship is given. Studies, 14ff.

6. From a structural point of view, Nicolo's private life occupies a weak position in terms of the novella's focus. Most of what occurs there is left in shadow for the reader and is only related and interpreted in broadest outline by the narrator. The emphasis in the story clearly rests on the relationships within the household. Hoverland advances an argument that Nicolo is not a central figure at all, that he functions as a catalyst in the story, causing a confrontation with Elvire's private "utopia" of Colino and is thus to be viewed structurally as an emanation from her sphere. Hoverland sees Elvire as the central figure, impenetrable even to the narrator, and the thrust of the story as the destruction of the unviable marital relationship and of the closed world in which Elvire lives. Hoverland's treatment of the pervasive imagery of keys provides good insight into the secrecy

and dynamics of the household, _Das Prinzip der Gestaltung_, 164ff.

Chapter 11. IDENTITY AND EXISTENCE

1. John Carl Blankenagel, in _The Dramas of Heinrich von Kleist_ (Chapel Hill: University of North Carolina Press, 1931), 153, however, sees Käthchen as the "embodiment of <Kleist's> human ideal of childlike simplicity, spontaneity, natural- ness, and youthful, unconscious charm and grace". Blankenagel equates her with the marionette. Käthchen displays a nearly total lack of personality, however, and as we are developing the argument here, this hardly represents Kleist's ideal state of anything.

2. Gert Ueding points out that Kunigunde also awakens mythological and dream-like associations, such as those of Eve, of Helen of Troy, and of Cleopatra, "Zweideutige Bilderwelt," 179.

3. R.D. Laing describes exactly this combination of anxieties in _The Divided Self_. Laing's term "ontological insecurity" is appropriate for Johann's sensitivity and fear.   Laing's discussion of anxiety responses includes "engulfment," "implosion," and the fear of "depersonalization," terms which fit Johann well, esp. 44f.

4. Friedrich Koch, _Bewußtsein und Wirklichkeit_, 163. Koch also points out that she is capable of living only in illusions because reality will not support her, 377.

5. Penthesilea's existential problems have been mentioned by other critics.   Paul Whitaker notes her fear of being a "thing" to Achilles' subject. "Penthesilea and the Problem of Bad Faith," _Colloquia Germanica_, 1972, 59-77. Whitaker applies Sartrean categories of description and judges Penthesilea to be living in bad faith in that, though she longs for love, she is "unwilling to risk the comfortable security of the Being-for-itself -- and attempting a dishonorable solution through bad faith she inevitably loses both <love and her Being-for-itself>"(77). Whitaker judges this to be a moral flaw in Penthesilea, however, and he bypasses her underlying and causal insecurity.   Ursula Mahlendorf's article, "The Wounded Self: Kleist's _Penthesilea_," _German Quarterly_, 52 (1979), 252-272, treats Penthesilea's weakness thoroughly and in many more facets, based on observations from various systems of psychoanalysis, than I have here, because this study is restricted primarily to aspects of interaction and the discrepancy between surface and content of the private reality which lies beneath.

6. The Elector in <u>Homburg</u> and certainly Hermann meet with success, of course, and even Kunigunde, insofar as she might go off to new and different adventures, is capable of succeeding. Kunigunde and the Elector do learn their limits, however. It is worth noting that the qualities which assist these characters in their respective successes -- an aloofness from others, a certainty of their own invulner-ability, motivations which do not stem from weakness -- make them ultimately seem more cruel than others of Kleist's characters. Most of the rest of Kleist's main characters who have been treated here do what they do for some defensive reason. Part of the reason the reader's sympathetic interest is drawn to them is the vulnerability that lies in their personality or in their situation.

7. Julietta's mother, it is interesting to note, turns the tables on the Commandant in a similar fashion. The Com-mandant's brusque control of what happens in the household proves no match for the shrewd insight which Julietta's mother brings to the situation. Initially she presents the very picture of a mindless conjugal appendage of Lorenzo, but as the story progresses she displays her mettle, and a wise mind is revealed to us. She is instrumental in bringing about the revelation of the truth -- through the ruse which she plays on the Marquise, taking the risk of losing her daughter in the very attempt to regain her; she is quite aware of what she is doing there and she is disconsolate into the evening, apologizing for her abuse of Julietta. She and Julietta are the ones who receive the Graf, and the Mother brings about the extravagant apology by the Commandant.

   Werner Krueger discusses roles and interpersonal dynamics in the family and argues that the family is reconstituted in the end after many changes in roles. The Commandant undergoes a crisis of legitmization after he abdicates or is forced out of the roles of father, husband, patriarch, and commandant; the Marquise realigns herself according to changes in her roles of married woman, daughter, mother, and masculine figure; the mother takes over control in the final scenes of the story, "Rolle und Rollenwechsel: Überlegungen zu Kleists <u>Marquise von O...</u>," <u>Acta Germanica</u>, 17 (1984), 29-51.

8. Similar to the reassertion of specific time relationships in the "Marquise" when the Graf and Julietta rejoin the world, mentioned above, Harro Müller notes in his discussion of <u>Homburg</u> a reassertion of specific time references into the text which coincide with Homburg's gaining of his inner equilibrium and with his entry into the real world. Harro Müller, "Die Zeitstruktur im Drama Heinrich von Kleists," Diss. Münster, 1964, 170f.

9. The situation is not entirely unambiguous, of course. When Homburg stands blindfolded in the courtyard awaiting his execution he smells flowers, and upon being offered

carnations he rather puzzlingly declares his intention to
take them home and place them in water. The many and
contradictory levels of consciousness on which Kleist's
characters operate simultaneously are apparent here. A part
of Homburg clearly still denies his impending death.

Chapter 12. PRIVATE WORLDS AND PUBLIC ROLES

1.   A few other critics take a more radical view than this.
     Wilhelm Emrich states that Kleist's art is only possible
     through "eine dem klassischen Denken unvorstellbare oder zum
     mindesten unerträgliche Destruktion der in und durch die
     Kunst dargestellten Weltwirklichkeit." "Kleist und die
     Moderne Literatur," in Heinrich von Kleist: Vier Reden zu
     seinem Gedächtnis, ed. Walter Müller-Seidel (Berlin: Erich
     Schmidt, 1962), 19. Emrich argues that Kleist achieves this
     radical departure from reality through "<die> Aufhebung aller
     außerpersonalen objektiven Eigengesetzlichkeiten," by which
     Emrich means laws of nature, history, and society. In place
     of this lost or destroyed reality, Emrich argues, Kleist
     endows his characters who have become self-conscious with a
     complete autonomy based on an absolute, infallible, and true
     internal law which Emrich, like Fricke, calls Gefühl. His
     former points are well taken, although Kleist seems less
     wedded to the idea of the power and solidity of the inner
     world than are many of his characters. This study has argued
     for a greater validity to the demands of the external world
     and for a greater fallibility of the individual's world.

2.   Erika Swales makes this last distinction in reference to the
     defensive and inflexible attitudes of the characters in the
     "Marquise," pointing out the functional distinction between
     "gebrechliche Welt" and "gebrechliche Einrichtung der Welt."
     "The Beleagured Citadel: A Study of Kleist's Die Marquise von
     O...," Deutsche Vierteljahresschrift für Literatur-
     wissenschaft und Geistesgeschichte, 51 (1977), esp. 131ff.
     The terms, which appear not only in the "Marquise," are used
     interchangeably by the narrator, but clearly the latter is
     what defines the problem.

3.   Also similar to this but on a less striking level, Eustache's
     "knowledge" that Rupert is not evil prevents her from seeing
     the evil that he is causing. In the way these characters
     positively skew their perception of the other person they are
     not unlike the characters who create a negative phantom out
     of another person, elevating another to the demonic rather
     than the divine, as Rupert does with his increasingly
     extravagant suspicions of Sylvester and as the Commandant
     does with Julietta when he thinks she has betrayed him. One
     might mention here as well Penthesilea's virtually infinite
     fear and then hatred of Achilles.

4. There occurs elsewhere in Kleist's works a great deal of saving that does not result in salvation, at least on a practical plane. Nicolo is saved by Piachi only to suffer a different kind of destruction; the Marquise's savior commits the same offense from which he had saved her; Villeneuve and Gustav surrender themselves to the very trap from which they thought they had been saved.

5. The possibility for Alkmene and Amphitryon to go through this process and thus see each other, really and for the first time, is not developed to that extent in the play, perhaps partly because of its origins as a translation of Moliere's Amphitryon.

6. The Graf is not set upon his course of self-discovery through manipulation or abuse by another character. In a sense, Kleist performs this function of alienating the Graf from himself by saddling him with the crime he could not have committed, much as the Graf does to Julietta.

SELECTED BIBLIOGRAPHY

Kleist, Heinrich von. Sämtliche Werke und Briefe. Ed. Helmut
    Sembdner. 6th ed. München: Hanser Verlag, 1977.

Aggeler, Jörg. Der Weg von Kleists Alkmene. Bern/Frankfurt:
    Herbert Lang/Peter Lang, 1972.

Altenhofer, Norbert. "Der erschütterte Sinn: Hermeneutische
    Überlegungen zu Kleists 'Das Erdbeben in Chili.'" Positionen
    der Literaturwissenschaft: Acht Modellanalysen am Beispiel
    von Kleists "Das Erdbeben in Chili." Ed. D. E. Wellbery.
    Munich: Beck, 1985. 39-53.

Arntzen, Helmut. "Drama der Bewußtseinsstufen: Heinrich von
    Kleist und 'Prinz Friedrich von Homburg." Zur Sprache
    Kommen: Studien zur Literatur- und Sprachreflexion, zur
    deutschen Literatur und zum öffentlichen Sprachgebrauch.
    Münster: Aschendorff, Münster Westfalen, 1983. 201-228.

Ayrault, Roger. Heinrich von Kleist. Paris: Montaigne, 1966.

Bab, Julius. Der Mensch auf der Bühne. Eine Dramaturgie für
    Schauspieler. Vol. 2. Berlin: Oesterfeld und Co., 1910.
    67-94.

Beckmann, Beat. Kleists Bewußtseinskritik: Eine Untersuchung der
    Erzählformen seiner Novellen. Bern: Peter Lang, 1978.

Belgardt, Raimund. "Kleists Weg zur Wahrheit: Irrtum und
    Wahrheit als Denkformen und Strukturmöglichkeiten."
    Zeitschrift für Deutsche Philologie 92 (1973): 161-184.

_____. "Prinz Friedrich von Homburgs Neues Wissen."
    Neophilologus 61 (1977): 100-110.

Bianchi, Lorenzo. "Die dramatische Kunstform bei Heinrich von
    Kleist." Studi di Filologia Moderna Jan.-June. 1914: 42-67.

Blankenagel, John Carl. The Dramas of Heinrich von Kleist: A
    Biographical and Critical Study. Chapel Hill: University of
    North Carolina, 1931.

232

Blöcker, Günther. _Heinrich von Kleist oder Das Absolute Ich_. Berlin: Argon, 1960.

Bochan, Bohdan. _The Phenomenology of Freedom in Kleist's "Die Familie Schroffenstein" and Penthesilea_." Frankfurt am Main: Peter Lang, 1982.

Böckmann, Paul. "Die Verrätselung des Daseins in Kleists Dichten." _Formensprache: Studien zur Literarästhetik und Dichtungsinterpretationen_. Hamburg: Hoffman and Campe, 1966. 385-406.

Brahm, Otto. _Heinrich von Kleist_. Berlin: Allgemeiner Verein für Deutsche Literatur, 1885.

Braig, Friedrich. _Heinrich von Kleist_. Munich: Beck, 1925.

Burckhardt, Sigurd. _The Drama of Language: Essays on Goethe and Kleist_. Baltimore: Johns Hopkins Press, 1970.

Cassirer, Ernst. _Heinrich von Kleist und die Kantische Philosophie_. Berlin: Reuther & Reichard, 1919.

Cohn, Dorrit. "Kleist's 'Marquise von O...': The Problem of Knowledge." _Monatshefte_ 67 (1975): 129-144.

Conrady, Karl Otto. "Das Moralische in Kleists Erzählungen: Ein Kapitel vom Dichter ohne Gesellschaft." _Literatur und Gesellschaft: vom neunzehnten ins zwangzigste Jahrhundert: Festschrift für Benno von Wiese_. Ed. Hans Joachim Schrimpf. Bonn: Bouvier, 1963. 56-82.

Corsson, Meta. _Kleist und Shakespeare_. Hildesheim: Gerstenberg, 1978.

Dietrick, Linda. _Prisons and Idylls: Studies in Heinrich von Kleist's Fictional World_. Frankfurt am Main: Peter Lang, 1985.

Dünnhaupt, Gerhard. "Kleist's _Marquise von O..._ and its Literary Debt to Cervantes." _Arcadia_ 10 (1975): 147-157.

Durzak, Manfred. "Zur Utopischen Funktion des Kindesbildes in Kleists Erzählungen." _Colloquia Germanica_ 1969: 111-129.

Dyck, J. W. "Heinrich von Kleist: Ehre und Ehrgeiz als Ursache der Schuld." _Husbanding the Golden Grain: Studies in Honor of Henry W. Nordmeyer_. Ed. Luanne T. Frank and Emery E. George. Ann Arbor: University of Michigan, 1973. 64-74.

Dyer, Denys G. "Kleist und das Paradoxe." _Kleistjahrbuch 1981/82_. Berlin: Erich Schmidt, 1983. 210-219.

Edel, Leon. The Modern Psychological Novel. New York: Grosset & Dunlap, 1964.

Ellis, John. Heinrich von Kleist: Studies in the Character and Meaning of his Writings. Chapel Hill: University of North Carolina, 1979.

_____. "Kleist's 'Der Zweikampf.'" Monatshefte 65 (1973): 48-60.

Emrich, Wilhelm. "Kleist und die Moderne Literatur." Heinrich von Kleist: Vier Reden zu seinem Gedächtnis. Ed. Walter Müller-Seidel. Berlin: Erich Schmidt, 1962. 9-25.

Ermattinger, Emil. Das dichterische Kunstwerk: Grundbegriffe der Urteilsbildung in der Literaturgeschichte. Leipzig/Berlin: Teubner, 1921.

Falkenfeld, Hellmuth. "Kant und Kleist." Logos 8.3 (1919): 303-319.

Fischer, Ernst. "Heinrich von Kleist." Heinrich von Kleist: Aufsätze und Essays. Ed. Walter Müller-Seidel. Darmstadt: Wissenschaftliche Buchgesellschaft, 1973. 459-552.

Frank, Luanne T. "Kleist's Achilles: Hilfskonstruktion or Hero?" Husbanding the Golden Grain: Studies in Honor of Henry W. Nordmeyer. Ed. Luanne T. Frank and Emery E. George. Ann Arbor: University of Michigan, 1973. 82-96.

Fricke, Gerhard. Gefühl und Schicksal bei Heinrich von Kleist. Berlin: Junker und Dünnhaupt, 1929.

_____. "Kleists 'Prinz von Homburg': Versuch einer Interpretation." Germanisch-Romanische Monatsschrift ns 2 (1951/52): 189-208.

_____. "Penthesilea." Das Deutsche Drama vom Barock bis zur Gegenwart. Ed. Benno von Wiese. Vol. 1. Düsseldorf: August Bagel, 1958. 363-384.

Gelus, Marjorie. "Displacement of Meaning: Kleist's 'Der Findling.'" German Quarterly 55 (1982): 541-553.

_____. "Laughter and Joking in the Works of Heinrich von Kleist." German Quarterly 50 (1977): 452-473.

Gilman, Sander L. "The Aesthetics of Blackness in Heinrich von Kleist's 'Die Verlobung in St. Domingo.'" MLN 90 (1975): 661-672.

Girard, Rene. "Mythos und Gegenmythos: Zu Kleists 'Das Erdbeben in Chili.'" Positionen der Literaturwissenschaft: Acht

Modellanalysen am Beispiel von Kleists "Das Erdbeben in Chili." Ed. D. E. Wellbery. Munich: Beck, 1985. 130-148.

Glicksberg, Charles Irving. _Modern Literary Perspectivism_. Dallas: Southern Methodist University Press, 1970.

Goffman, Erving. _The Presentation of Self in Everyday Life_. New York: Doubleday Anchor, 1959.

_____. _Where the Action Is_. London: Allen Lane's The Penguin Press, 1969.

Graham, Ilse Appelbaum. "The Broken Pitcher: Hero of Kleist's Comedy." _Modern Language Quarterly_ 16 (1955): 99-113.

_____. _Heinrich von Kleist: Word into Flesh: A Poet's Quest for the Symbol_. Berlin, New York: de Gruyter, 1977.

Gundolf, Friedrich. _Heinrich von Kleist_. Leipzig: Hesse und Becker, 1922.

Harlos, Dieter. _Die Gestaltung psychischer Konflikte einiger Frauengestalten im Werk Heinrich von Kleists_. Frankfurt am Main: Peter Lang, 1984.

Heine, Roland. "'Ein Traum, was sonst?': Zum Verhältnis von Traum und Wirklichkeit in Kleists 'Prinz Friedrich von Homburg.'" _Literaturwissenschaft und Geistesgeschichte: Festschrift für Richard Brinkman_. Ed. Jürgen Brummack et. al. Tübingen: Max Niemeyer Verlag, 1981. 283-313.

Heiseler, Bernt von. "Kleist und seine Sprachkunst." _Ahnung und Aussage: Essays_. Gütersloh: C. Bertelsmann, 1952.

Helbling, Robert E. _The Major Works of Heinrich von Kleist_. New York: New Directions, 1975.

Herrmann, Hans Peter. "Zufall und Ich: Zum Begriff der Situation in den Novellen Heinrich von Kleists." _Germanisch-Romanische Monatsschrift_ ns 11 (1961): 69-99.

Herzog, Wilhelm. _Heinrich von Kleist: Sein Leben und sein Werk_. Munich: Beck, 1911.

Hoffmann, Sven Olaf. "Das Identitätsproblem in Heinrich von Kleists _Penthesilea._" _Psychoanalytische Textinterpretationen_. Ed. Johannes Cremerius. Hamburg: Hoffmann und Campe, 1974. 172-180.

Hoffmeister, Elmar. _Täuschung und Wirklichkeit bei Heinrich von Kleist_. Bonn: H. Bouvier, 1968.

Hoffmeister, Johannes. "Beitrag zur sogenannten Kantkrise Heinrich von Kleists." _Deutsche Vierteljahresschrift für_

Literaturwissenschaft und Geistesgeschichte 33 (1959): 574-587.

Hoffmeister, Werner. "Heinrich von Kleists 'Findling.'" Monatshefte 58 (1966): 49-63.

Hohoff, Curt. Komik und Humor bei Heinrich von Kleist: Ein Beitrag zur Klärung der geistigen Struktur eines Dichters. Germanische Studien. Pt. 184, 1937.

_____. "Traum und Wirklichkeit bei Heinrich von Kleist." Merkur 15 (1961): 1026-1034.

Holz, Hans Heinz. Macht und Ohnmacht der Sprache: Untersuchungen zum Sprachverständnis und Stil Heinrich von Kleists. Frankfurt: Athenäum, 1962.

Horn, P. "Hatte Kleist Rassenvorurteile? Eine kritische Auseinandersetzung mit der Literatur zu 'Verlobung in St. Domingo.'" Monatshefte 67 (1975): 117-128.

Hoverland, Lilian. Heinrich von Kleist und das Prinzip der Gestaltung. Königstein/Ts.: Scriptor, 1978.

Hubbs, Valentine C. "Die Ambiguität in Kleists 'Prinz Friedrich von Homburg.'" Kleist Jahrbuch 1981/82. Berlin: Erich Schmidt, 1983. 184-194.

_____. "Die Romantische Mythe der Transformation in den Werken Heinrich von Kleists." Husbanding the Golden Grain: Studies in Honor of Henry W. Nordmeyer. Ed. Luanne T. Frank and Emery E. George. Ann Arbor: University of Michigan, 1973. 169-178.

Huizinga, J. Homo Ludens: A Study of the Play-Element in Culture. London: Routledge & Kegan Ltd., 1949.

Ide, Heinz. Der Junge Kleist. Würzburg: Holzner, 1961.

Jancke, Gerhard. "Zum Problem des identischen Selbst in Kleists Lustspiel Amphitryon." Colloquia Germanica 1969: 87-110.

Kaim, Rudolf. Der Sinn der Literaturwissenschaft. Philosophische Reihe 41. Munich: Rösl & Cie, 1921.

Kaiser, Gerhard. "Mythos und Person in Kleists 'Penthesilea.'" Wandrer und Idylle: Goethe und die Phänomenologie der Natur in der deutschen Dichtung von Geßner bis Gottfried Keller. Göttingen: Vandenhoeck & Ruprecht, 1977. 209-239.

Kayser, Wolfgang. "Kleist als Erzähler." German Life & Letters 8 (1954): 19-29.

236

Kindermann, Heinz. "Kleist und Grillparzer." <u>Meister der</u>
<u>Komödie</u>: <u>Von Aristophanes bis</u> G.B. <u>Shaw</u>. Vienna/Munich:
Donau-Verlag, 1952. 231-241.

Klein, Johannes. <u>Die Geschichte der Deutschen Novelle von Goethe</u>
<u>bis zur Gegenwart</u>. Wiesbaden: F. Steiner, 1954.

Kluge, Gerhard. "Der Wandel der dramatischen Konzeption von der
'Familie Ghonorez' zur 'Familie Schroffenstein.'" <u>Kleists</u>
<u>Dramen</u>: <u>Neue Interpretationen</u>. Ed. Walter Hinderer.
Stuttgart: Reclam, 1981. 52-72.

Koch, Friedrich. <u>Heinrich von Kleist</u>: <u>Bewußtsein und Wirklich-</u>
<u>keit</u>. Stuttgart: Metzler and Carl Ernst Poeschel, 1958.

Kohrs, Ingrid. <u>Das Wesen des Tragischen im Drama Heinrichs von</u>
<u>Kleist</u>: <u>Dargestellt an Interpretationen von</u> "<u>Penthesilea</u>"
<u>und</u> "<u>Prinz Friedrich von</u> Homburg." Marburg/Lahn: Simons
Verlag, 1951.

Kommerell, Max. "Die Sprache und das Unaussprechliche: Eine
Betrachtung über Heinrich von Kleist." <u>Geist und Buchstabe</u>
<u>der Dichtung</u>: <u>Goethe</u>, <u>Schiller</u>, <u>Kleist</u>, <u>Hölderlin</u>. 4th ed.
Frankfurt: Klostermann, 1956. 243-317.

Koopmann, Helmut. "Das 'Rätselhafte Faktum' und seine
Vorgeschichte: Zum analytischen Charakter der Novellen
Heinrich von Kleists." <u>Zeitschrift für Deutsche Philologie</u>
84 (1965): 508-550.

Korff, Hermann August. <u>Geist der Goethezeit</u>. <u>Versuch einer</u>
<u>Ideelen Entwicklung der klassisch-romantischen Literatur-</u>
<u>geschichte</u>. Pt. 4, Hochromantik. Leipzig: Koehler &
Ameland, 1953. 47-92, 272-314.

Krueger, Werner. "Rolle und Rollenwechsel: Überlegungen zu
Kleists "'Marquise von O...'" <u>Acta Germanica</u> 17 (1984):
29-51.

Kunz, Josef. <u>Die deutsche Novelle zwischen Klassik und Romantik</u>.
2nd edition. Berlin: Erich Schmidt, 1971.

_____. "Die Thematik der Daseinsstufen in Kleists
Dichterischem Werk." Festvortrag an der Philipps-Universität
Marburg aus Anlaß des 150. Todestages des Dichters. <u>Heinrich</u>
<u>von Kleist</u>: <u>Aufsätze und Essays</u>. Ed. Walter Müller- Seidel.
Darmstadt: Wissenschaftliche Buchgesellschaft, 1973.
672-706.

Kurz, Gerhard. "'Gott Befohlen:' Kleists Dialog 'Über das
Marionettentheater' und der Mythos vom Sündenfall des
Bewußtseins." <u>Kleist Jahrbuch 1981/82</u>. Berlin: Erich
Schmidt, 1983. 264-277.

Labhardt, Robert. Metapher und Geschichte: Kleists dramatische Metaphorik bis zur "Penthesilea" als Widerspiegelung seiner geschichtlichen Position. Kronberg/Ts.: Scriptor, 1976.

Laing, R.D. The Divided Self: An Existential Study in Sanity and Madness. London: Tavistock, 1969.

_____. Self and Others. London: Tavistock, 1969.

Laurs, Axel. "Narrative Strategy in Heinrich von Kleists 'Die Heilige Cäcilie oder Die Gewalt der Musik.'" Journal of the Australasian Universities Language and Literature Association 60 (1983): 220-233.

Lukacs, Georg. "Die Tragödie Heinrich von Kleists." In Deutsche Realisten des neunzehnten Jahrhunderts. Berlin: Aufbau-Verlag, 1951. 19-48.

Mahlendorf, Ursula R. "The Wounded Self: Kleist's Penthesilea." German Quarterly 52 (1979): 252-277.

Mathieu, G. "Kleist's Hermann: The Portrait of an Artist in Propaganda." German Life & Letters ns 7 (1953/54): 1-10.

May, Kurt. "Kleists 'Hermannsschlacht': Eine Strukturanalyse." Form und Bedeutung: Interpretationen deutscher Dichtung des 18. und 19. Jahrhunderts. Stuttgart: E. Klett, 1957. 254-262.

_____. "Kleists 'Penthesilea.'" Form und Bedeutung: Interpretationen deutscher Dichtung des 18. und 19. Jahrhunderts. Stuttgart: E. Klett, 1957. 243-253.

McGlathery, James M. Desire's Sway: The Plays and Stories of Heinrich von Kleist. Detroit: Wayne State University Press, 1983.

Moering, Michael. Witz und Ironie in der Prosa Heinrich von Kleists. Munich: Wilhelm Fink, 1972.

Moore, Erna. "Heinrich von Kleists 'Findling': Psychologie des Verhängnisses." Colloquia Germanica 1974: 275-297.

Müller, Harro. "Die Zeitstruktur im Drama Heinrich von Kleists." Diss. Münster, 1964.

Müller, Joachim. "Zufall und Vorfall: Geschehenswelt und Erzähl-struktur in Heinrich von Kleists Novelle Der Findling." Zeitschrift für Germanistik 4 (1982): 427-438.

Müller-Salget, Klaus. "Das Prinzip der Doppeldeutigkeit in Kleists Erzählungen." Zeitschrift für Deutsche Philologie 92 (1973): 185-211.

Müller-Seidel, Walter, ed. Heinrich von Kleist: Aufsätze und Essays. Darmstadt: Wissenschaftliche Buchgesellschaft, 1973.

_____. "Heinrich von Kleist und die Wahrheit des Menschen." Stoffe, Formen, Strukturen: Studien zur Deutschen Literatur. Hans Heinrich Borcherdt zum 75. Geburtstag. Munich: Hueber, 1962. 331-344.

_____. "Prinz Friedrich von Homburg." Das Deutsche Drama vom Barock bis zur Gegenwart. Ed. Benno von Wiese. Vol. 1. Düsseldorf: August Bagel, 1958. 385-404.

_____. "Die Struktur des Widerspruchs in Kleists 'Marquise von O...'" Deutsche Vierteljahresschrift für Literaturwissenschaft und Geistesgeschichte 28 (1954): 497-515.

_____. "Die Vermischung des Komischen mit dem Tragischen in Kleists Lustspiel 'Amphitryon.'" Jahrbuch der Deutschen Schillergesellschaft 5 (1961): 118-135.

_____. Versehen und Erkennen: Eine Studie über Heinrich von Kleist. Cologne: Böhlau, 1961.

Muth, Ludwig. Kleist und Kant: Versuch einer neuen Interpretation." Cologne: Kölner Universitätsverlag, 1954.

Ohmann, Fritz. "Kleist und Kant." Festschrift für B. Litzmann zum 60. Gegurtstag, 18.4.1917. Im Auftrage der Literarhistorischen Gesellschaft Bonn. Ed. Carl Enders. Bonn: Cohen, 1920. 105-131.

Politzer, Heinz. "Der Fall der Frau Marquise: Beobachtungen zu Kleists Die Marquise von O..." Deutsche Vierteljahresschrift für Literaturwissenschaft und Geistesgeschichte 51 (1977): 98-128.

Reske, Hermann. "Die Kleistische Sprache." German Quarterly 36 (1963): 219-235.

Rieger, Bernhard. Geschlechterrollen und Familienstrukturen in den Erzählungen Heinrich von Kleists. Frankfurt am Main: Peter Lang, 1985.

Rottenbiller, Henry. "Metaphorik der psychogenen Kausalität in der Dichtung Heinrich von Kleists." Diss. Michigan State University, 1971. DAI 32 (1971/72), 1527A.

Schlueter, June. Metafictional Characters in Modern Drama. New York: Columbia University, 1979.

Schmidt, Jochen. Heinrich von Kleist: Studien zu seiner poetischen Verfahrensweise. Tübingen: Max Niemeyer Verlag, 1974.

Schmidt, Wieland, ed. Die Gegenwärtigkeit Kleists: Reden zum Gedenkjahr 1977 im Schloß Charlottenburg zu Berlin. Berlin: Erich Schmidt Verlag, 1980.

Schneider, Karl Ludwig. "Heinrich von Kleist: über ein Ausdrucksprinzip seines Stils." Libris et litteris. Festschrift für Hermann Tiemann zum 60. Geburtstag am 9. Juli 1959. Ed. Christian Voigt and Erich Zimmermann. Hamburg: Maximilian-Gesellschaft, 1959. 258-271.

Schrimpf, Hans Joachim. "Tragedy and Comedy in the Works of Heinrich von Kleist." Monatshefte 58 (1966): 193-208.

_____. "Der Zerbrochne Krug." Das Deutsche Drama vom Barock bis zur Gegenwart. Ed. Benno von Wiese. Vol. 1. Düsseldorf: August Bagel, 1958. 339-362.

Schwerte, Hans. "Das Käthchen von Heilbronn." Der Deutsch-unterricht 13.2 (1961): 5-26.

Scott, D.F.S. "Heinrich von Kleist's Kant Crisis." Modern Language Review 42 (1947): 474-484.

Seeba, Hinrich C. "Der Sündenfall des Verdachts: Identitätskrise und Sprachskepsis in Kleists 'Familie Schroffenstein.'" Deutsche Vierteljahresschrift für Literaturwissenschaft und Geistesgeschichte 44 (1970): 64-100.

Seidlin, Oskar. "What the Bell Tolls in Kleist's Der Zerbrochene Krug." Deutsche Vierteljahresschrift für Literatur-wissenschaft und Geistesgeschichte 51 (1977): 78-97.

Skrotzki, Ditmar. Die Gebärde des Errötens im Werk Heinrich von Kleists. Marburg: N.G. Elwert, 1971.

Stahl, E.L. Heinrich von Kleist's Dramas. Oxford: Blackwell, 1948.

Staiger, Emil. "Kleist: Das Bettelweib von Locarno." Meister-werke Deutscher Sprache. 4th ed. Zurich: Atlantis, 1961. 100-117.

Stefansky, Georg. "Ein Neuer Weg zu Heinrich von Kleist." Euphorion 23.4 (1921): 639-694.

Stephens, Anthony. "The Illusion of a Shaped World: Kleist and Tragedy." Journal of the Australasian Universities Language and Literature Association 60 (Nov. 1983): 197-219.

_____. "'Was hilfts, dass ich jetzt schuldlos mich erzähle': Zur Bedeutung der Erzählvorgänge in Kleists Dramen." Jahrbuch der Deutschen Schillergesellschaft 29 (1985): 301- 303.

Stierle, Karlheinz. "Das Beben des Bewußtseins: Die Narrative Struktur von Kleists 'Das Erdbeben in Chili.'" Positionen der Literaturwissenschaft: Acht Modellanalysen am Beispiel von Kleists "Das Erdbeben in Chili." Ed. D. E. Wellbery. Munich: Beck, 1985. 54-68.

Swales, Erika. "The Beleaguered Citadel: A Study of Kleist's Die Marquise von O...." Deutsche Vierteljahresschrift für Literaturwissenschift und Geistesgeschichte 51 (1977): 129-147.

Thalmann, Marianne. "Das Jupiterspiel in Kleists Amphitryon." Maske und Kothurn 9 (1963): 56-67.

Tymms, Ralph. "Alternation of Personality in the Dramas of Heinrich von Kleist and Zacharias Werner." Modern Language Review 37 (1942): 64-73.

_____. Doubles in Literary Psychology. Cambridge: Bowes & Bowes, 1949.

Ueding, Gert. "Zweideutige Bilderwelt: 'Das Kätchen von Heilbronn.'" Kleists Dramen: Neue Interpretationen. Stuttgart: Reclam, 1981. 172-187.

Ugrinsky, Alexej, Frederick J. Churchill, Frank S. Lambasca, & Robert F. von Berg, eds. Heinrich von Kleist-Studien. Berlin: Erich Schmidt Verlag, 1980.

Weigand, Hermann J. "Das Vertrauen als Zentralbegriff in Heinrich von Kleists Dramatik." and "Das Vertrauen in Kleists Erzählungen." Fährten und Funde: Aufsätze zur Deutschen Literatur. Bern: Francke, 1967. 72-84, 85-119.

_____. "Zu Kleists Käthchen von Heilbronn." Studia Philologica et Litteraria in Honorem L. Spitzer. Ed. A.G. Hatcher and K.L. Selig. Bern: Francke, 1958. 413-430.

Wells, G. A.. "The Limitations of Knowledge: Kleist's 'Über das Marionettentheater.'" Modern Language Review 80.1 (1985): 90-96.

Weiss, Hermann F. "Precarious Idylls. The Relationship Between Father and Daughter in Heinrich von Kleist's Die Marquise von O...." MLN 91 (1976): 538-42.

Whitaker, Paul K. "Penthesilea and the Problem of Bad Faith." Colloquia Germanica 1972: 59-77.

Wiese, Benno von. Die Deutsche Tragödie von Lessing bis Hebbel. Vol. 2. Hamburg: Hoffmann und Campe, 1948. 15-102.

Witkop, Philipp. Heinrich von Kleist. Leipzig: H. Haesel, 1922.

Wittkowski, Wolfgang. "Die Verschleierung der Wahrheit in und über Kleists _Amphitryon_: Zur dialektischen Aufhebung eines Lustspiels oder über den neuen mystischen Amphitryon und dergleichen Zeichen der Zeit." _Wahrheit und Sprache_: _Festschrift für Bert Nagel_. Ed. Wilhelm Pelters and Paul Schimmelpfennig. Göppingen: Alfred Kümmerle, 1972. 151-170.

Wolff, Hans M. _Heinrich von Kleist als Politischer Dichter_. University of California Publications in Modern Philology, 27.6. Berkeley: University of California, 1947. 343-521.

_____. _Heinrich von Kleist_: _Die Geschichte seines Schaffens_. Bern: Francke, 1954.

INDEX

Edith Borchardt

MYTHISCHE STRUKTUREN IM WERK HEINRICH VON KLEISTS

American University Studies: Series I (Germanic Languages and Literature). Vol. 40
ISBN 0-8204-0457-8   250 pages   hardback US $ 38.50*

*Recommended price - alterations reserved

This book deals exclusively with the problem of androgyny in Kleist's life and work and attempts to explain his premature ecstatic death with Henriette Vogel on the basis of patterns of male/female relationships which become apparent in a detailed structural analysis of several of his works, revealing the archetype of the androgyne on both a literary and personal level. Borchardt uses an interdisciplinary approach based on Jungian aesthetics and Mauron's psychocriticism. Psychological and anthropological theories help to explain the process of *biopoesis:* how a mental image takes on concrete expression in language, and how the symbol becomes a container for psychic energy. Finally, this revealing study relates psychic and mythic structures in Kleist's work to similar patterns in his life and analyzes the archetype of the androgyne and the hermaphrodite as they reflect the processes of creativity.

«I am recommending to you for publication an important study in which the problem of androgyny in Kleist is treated for the first time through a dynamic analysis for Jungian symbolic structures rather than a static taxonomy»
(Hinrich C. Seeba, University of California, Berkeley)

«... an original contribution».
(James L. Larson, University of California, Berkeley)

 PETER LANG PUBLISHING, INC.
62 West 45th Street
USA - New York, NY 10036